Praise for

"Must have information for busines[s] [executives]...
Boston Capital Ventures

"What C-Level executives read to keep their edge and make pivotal business decisions. Timeless classics for indispensable knowledge." - Richard Costello, Manager-Corporate Marketing Communication, General Electric

"Want to know what the real leaders are thinking about now? It's in here." - Carl Ledbetter, SVP & CTO, Novell, Inc.

"Great information for both novices and experts." - Patrick Ennis, Partner, ARCH Venture Partners

"Priceless wisdom from experts at applying technology in support of business objectives." - Frank Campagnoni, CTO, GE Global Exchange Services

"Unique insights into the way the experts think and the lessons they've learned from experience." - MT Rainey, Co-CEO, Young & Rubicam/Rainey Kelly Campbell Roalfe

"A must read for anyone in the industry." - Dr. Chuck Lucier, Chief Growth Officer, Booz-Allen & Hamilton

"Unlike any other business books, Inside the Minds captures the essence, the deep-down thinking processes, of people who make things happen." - Martin Cooper, CEO, Arraycomm

"A must read for those who manage at the intersection of business and technology." - Frank Roney, General Manager, IBM

"A great way to see across the changing marketing landscape at a time of significant innovation." - David Kenny, Chairman & CEO, Digitas

"An incredible resource of information to help you develop outside-the-box..." - Rich Jernstedt, CEO, Golin/Harris International

"A snapshot of everything you need to know..." - Larry Weber, Founder, Weber Shandwick

"The only useful way to get so many good minds speaking on a complex topic." - Scott Bradner, Senior Technical Consultant, Harvard University

www.Aspatore.com

Aspatore Books is the largest and most exclusive publisher of C-Level executives (CEO, CFO, CTO, CMO, Partner) from the world's most respected companies and law firms. Aspatore annually publishes a select group of C-Level executives from the Global 1,000, top 250 law firms (Partners and Chairs), and other leading companies of all sizes. C-Level Business Intelligence™, as conceptualized and developed by Aspatore Books, provides professionals of all levels with proven business intelligence from industry insiders – direct and unfiltered insight from those who know it best – as opposed to third-party accounts offered by unknown authors and analysts. Aspatore Books is committed to publishing an innovative line of business and legal books, those which lay forth principles and offer insights that when employed, can have a direct financial impact on the reader's business objectives, whatever they may be. In essence, Aspatore publishes critical tools – need-to-read as opposed to nice-to-read books – for all business professionals.

Inside the Minds

The critically acclaimed *Inside the Minds* series provides readers of all levels with proven business intelligence from C-Level executives (CEO, CFO, CTO, CMO, Partner) from the world's most respected companies. Each chapter is comparable to a white paper or essay and is a future-oriented look at where an industry/profession/topic is heading and the most important issues for future success. Each author has been carefully chosen through an exhaustive selection process by the *Inside the Minds* editorial board to write a chapter for this book. *Inside the Minds* was conceived in order to give readers actual insights into the leading minds of business executives worldwide. Because so few books or other publications are actually written by executives in industry, *Inside the Minds* presents an unprecedented look at various industries and professions never before available.

INSIDE THE MINDS

Venture Capital
Best Practices

*Leading Venture Capitalists & Lawyers Offer
a Behind-the-Scenes Perspective on Doing Deals*

Published by Aspatore, Inc.

For corrections, company/title updates, comments or any other inquiries please email info@aspatore.com.

First Printing, 2005
10 9 8 7 6 5 4 3 2 1

ISBN 1-59622-035-X Library of Congress Control Number: 2005927548

Inside the Minds Managing Editor, Laura Kearns, Edited by Michaela Falls

Venture Capital
Best Practices

*Leading Venture Capitalists & Lawyers Offer
a Behind-the-Scenes Perspective on Doing Deals*

CONTENTS

View from a Veteran Venture Investor Reentering the Business Today

Joe Horowitz

Managing General Partner
JAFCO Ventures

Joe Horowitz, Managing General Partner of JAFCO Ventures, is a veteran venture capitalist who formally reentered the venture capital business in June of 2003. The following chapter is about Joe's views of the venture capital industry upon his reentry and some of his observations about building a successful venture firm in today's challenging environment.

Today's Venture Business

Fundamentally, the venture capital business is a very difficult business. Even for talented venture capitalists, the vagaries of the market can influence outcomes more than all of the effort in the world. Although some have tried to institutionalize venture capital, it is still an individual craftsman business, making it very difficult to scale. It all seems so complicated, but in truth the basic proposition is fairly simple: invest in newly formed companies, help them out, hope that they produce a positive liquidity event, and when you add it all up, create a great return for your limited partners. Just because it is simple to describe, however, does not mean that it is easy to do well and in fact, relatively few people have had consistent success in the business. None of this is earth-shattering news; it is just that the Internet-bubble made it look far too easy. But now that the world has sobered, we are back to the basics, which means back to the hard work and the difficult task of figuring it out one step at a time.

In the early period of the post-Internet bubble era, many limited partners of venture firms expressed great concern about the lack of new investment activity. Particularly in light of large fund sizes, they worried that many successful venture capitalists were not fully engaged and working as hard as they could. In my opinion, the post-Internet transition period was very rocky for everyone in the business, difficult in the extreme, and emotionally draining. New venture activity was quite low because market directions were unclear and much time was spent sorting out existing portfolio companies. Having spent time with many top-tier venture capitalists since my re-entry into the business, it is clear that venture capitalists today are very rejuvenated. I believe that venture capitalists, particularly among the top-tier firms, take a lot of pride in the value and reputation of their franchises. They are applying their years of experience to interesting, well thought-out new ventures, and are as determined as ever to win. These are the people who have "been to the movie" many times before and know what it takes to succeed at a grand level. They carefully measure the risk of wasting capital before engaging in a project. They fully appreciate the commitment of time associated with sponsoring a new company, and as a result they do not help launch a venture without feeling highly confident of the potential for breakout success. I firmly believe that we will see the benefits of the venture investments from top-tier firms for a long time to come.

Perhaps the most startling change that I have observed during my re-entry into the venture capital business is the sheer number of funds and the aggregate amount of capital available for investment. When I first entered the venture business in the late 1970s, we were evolving from a "club" to a cottage industry at best. Most leading firms tried to work together, to share financing risks, and to improve deal flow through reciprocity: "I will show you some of my best deals in exchange for you showing me some of yours." We all knew each other, and the venture capital community was small enough that even as late as the mid-1980s all of our names could fit on one chart. (In 1984 Asset Management put together a diagram showing the history of all of the west coast venture capital investors on a single poster.) When fund sizes grew above the $100 million mark, many of us struggled to imagine how we would be able to create superior returns with such vast amounts of capital to invest. In sharp contrast, today it seems that the number of new funds and the volume of capital are almost without bound. If size is the determinant of an industry, the venture capital business truly is a full-fledged industry.

How this came about is fairly clear. The Internet bubble begot capital needs that grew exponentially, precipitating the opportunity for larger funds and many more of them. With the success of so many venture-backed companies, many more limited partners became interested in the asset class. The barriers to entry in the venture business fell dramatically, but then, when the environment changed after the bubble collapsed, even marginal firms continued. Unlike businesses that can disappear in an instant, venture firms are structured around funds with ten-year contractual commitments. Thus, today we have a clear imbalance of too much capital supply to legitimate venture demand that I fear will negatively impact returns for the venture capital industry as a whole. Although many participants in the venture business share this view, I do not believe that this will be the case for the top-tier firms and for those firms with well-defined, differentiated business models. Rather, I believe these funds will prosper and serve their limited partners well.

Top-tier firms are top tier for a reason. They consist of very smart people who know what they are doing and leverage their franchise value well. They also have recognized and properly reacted to the changing venture capital climate by reducing fund sizes and trimming their businesses accordingly. These are the firms that have the experience to deliver results, and know how to attract the highest-quality venture deals. It is especially true today that the most talented entrepreneurs see the value of working with top-tier firms to help them achieve their goals and resist working with less experienced venture capitalists. It is not just about capital and valuation, but contacts and experience. In my view, this trend will result in a further bifurcation of the returns of these firms relative to the industry as a whole. In many ways, this prediction is not particularly surprising since historically, the top-tier venture firms have consistently been responsible for a disproportionate number of the greatest successes of the venture capital business and the highest returns for their limited partners.

So where does that leave the vast number of other venture capital firms in the industry? I think the answer is clear; eventually, many of them will go away. Just as in any business, if a new venture cannot adequately answer basic questions such as the market it serves, its differentiation, and competitive advantage, one should question why it should be in business at all. I believe that over time limited partners will hold venture capital firms to the same criteria.

Have a Differentiated Strategy

It all comes down to relevance. Given the finite universe of quality deals relative to an abundance of capital, if a venture capital firm cannot demonstrate its relevance, the risk of unnatural investment behavior will likely increase. For example, less differentiated firms will tend to overpay for deals or provide capital to companies that are less deserving. When this occurs, more capital is wasted on failed companies. In addition, emerging markets can be damaged by too many entrants. As a result, venture returns overall will suffer.

So how do firms that are not recognized as top-tier franchises deal with the issue of strategic differentiation? The answer lies in the most overused term in venture capital—"value-add." The value-added proposition of a venture capital firm must be at the heart of its existence and its strategic differentiation. With many seasoned venture investors, a firm's value-added proposition needs to be more than having been a successful entrepreneur in the past or offering to be another hardworking, smart voice around the table. As a starting point, to be successful in today's venture capital world, a firm's value-added proposition has to be very real, very tangible, and address a well-perceived need in the market.

There are many good examples of legitimate, differentiated strategies in the venture business. Some firms adopt a regional focus. Others build an expertise in a stage of investing or a specific layer of the capital structure. Still others are pure industry plays supported by tremendous domain knowledge. Ultimately a venture firm's success depends on the quality of the team and its execution, but a firm also must have a solid business model built upon a distinct core competency.

The opportunity to build a venture capital business around a differentiated strategy was central to my decision to join JAFCO Ventures. If I had not viewed the market need for JAFCO's value-added proposition as compelling, I would not have joined the firm.

JAFCO Ventures has developed an impressive legacy of helping U.S. technology ventures build sales and distribution channels in Japan with an Asia-based business development team and process. The firm has a long history of being involved with many great venture deals because of this capability, resulting in exceptional returns for their limited partners. It also seemed clear that the value of building a strong Asia presence for many venture-backed companies is more important than ever before.

The concept of this approach was originally pioneered by JAFCO's investment team in the early 1990s, a group that subsequently spun out to form Worldview Technology Partners. And while there are other venture firms that have subsequently emerged with similar Asia-oriented strategies, our view at JAFCO today is to collaborate with them since we believe it will lead to greater success for everyone.

Define your Business Model

For any venture firm, it is important to define a business model around a unique competence and to determine a stage of investing that is consistent with that strategy. The investment stage focus is also of particular importance since it affects how a firm approaches deal flow, competitors, and execution issues.

At JAFCO Ventures, we define our business model around our core competence in Asia since it is central to our differentiated, value-added proposition. When we considered defining our stage of investment focus, we noted that the optimal time for most new companies to benefit from our Asia capabilities was at their expansion-stage of development as they considered markets globally. Reaching this stage tended to coincide with their second or third round of financing. Logically, we considered the investment stage focus of our business model as the Series B or C financing.

Conventional wisdom regarding stage strategies is that the seed and early stage investors can produce great returns by securing significant ownership in companies that evolve into big hits, but successfully attracting start-up deals with true breakout potential is increasingly difficult for all but the top-tier firms. At the other end of the spectrum, later-stage investors place capital in more mature ventures and can produce strong results from an internal rate of return (or IRR) perspective, but their performance is also based upon public market timing risks. Investing at the early expansion-stage can be particularly difficult unless one exercises a lot of discipline, for although the venture may seem less risky overall, there are still many execution challenges ahead and the rash investor can be easily disappointed. Multi-stage investing often translates into putting money to work across many sectors at every stage, although many multi-stage funds are evolving with a bias toward one end of the spectrum or the other.

After weighing the possibilities at JAFCO Ventures, we decided that it made the most sense to define ourselves as pure early expansion-stage investors for the following reasons:

- JAFCO Ventures had a proven track record as a highly successful, early expansion-stage investor, in part because of the skill of its business development resources in evaluating new product/technology trends globally. By leveraging this expertise, we felt we had a unique understanding of how to assess risks at this stage of investing.

- By defining second and third round financings as the focus of our business, we would send a message to top-tier and other quality, early stage venture capital firms that we were not competing against them, but looking to complement them.

- Entrepreneurs tend to perceive the importance of their Asia strategy prior to their early expansion-stage capital needs; thus we could potentially gain an early look at deals and compete effectively based on our Asia value proposition and deep knowledge of the venture process.

In essence, we believed that by defining our business model around an Asia business development competence and an early expansion-stage investment orientation, we would have access to some of the best emerging ventures, sponsored by the most talented people in the venture business.

Having defined those aspects of our business model, the final major element to assess was the optimal fund size. As we all have learned, fund size should not be driven by the amount one can raise, but by the amount that can be optimally deployed. Fund size is also key to determining the average size of initial investments, which is an important factor in structuring financings and dealing with other investors. In this regard, we had a clear bias toward a smaller fund size. Venture capital firms with smaller funds will not pressure companies to raise too much capital, can be more selective in choosing investment opportunities, and are better positioned to maximize returns for limited partners. We determined that our ideal fund size, based upon creating a portfolio of about thirty companies with initial average investments of $4 to 6 million, was $200 million. We were therefore very pleased to start out with $100 million in our first fund to prove our business model with a new team.

In my view, a venture capital firm must deliberate these major components of the business model, value-add, focus, and fund size to determine what business it is in and how it can best serve limited partners. Once defined, it is equally important that a venture firm does not drift from its business model unless it represents a conscious, necessary decision based on a perceived change in the market. Often a change of focus occurs for the wrong reasons, such as an increase in fund size or a lack of investment discipline. The consequences of such loss of focus can be significant since the business model should be the foundation of the venture firm's organizational structure and operations.

Develop an Operating Paradigm that Complements Your Business Model

In today's venture capital business, as in the past, the talent of a firm's investment team is the primary driver of a fund's performance. However, organizational structure and process can have a significant impact on results and must be in tune with the venture firm's business model.

Traditional start-up venture capital firms are typically organized around the skills and efforts of their general partners. This structure makes a great deal of sense since early stage venture investors are individual craftsmen, operating in a world that requires great vision and foresight. In many ways, it would be sub-optimal to constrain a general partner's ability to think or act by imposing excessive process. In such firms, process is more geared to facilitate communication and collaboration. Although most early stage venture firms are very team-oriented, they are analogous to golf teams, in that each professional hopes to post strong enough individual scores to produce great results collectively.

By comparison, venture firms with other types of business models may require very different operating paradigms. For example, JAFCO Ventures, as a pure early expansion-stage investor, adopted an investment thesis less about embracing a vision for a company, and more about testing its validity in terms of product acceptance and market readiness. As a result, we designed our organizational structure and processes to be specific to our stage of investing. We developed systems to track investment opportunities that we consider relevant to our business model. We have tools that measure our performance along a number of metrics ranging from the share of deals in our target market that we were able to evaluate, to the speed of our investment decision process. Organizationally, we always operate as a team to be responsive to a company and thorough in our deal evaluation. Virtually every member of our investment and business development teams plays a role in evaluating each serious investment opportunity. In contrast to most early stage venture firms, our style of execution looks more like a basketball team than a golf team. We believe that how we play together affects our performance far more than how well we contribute individually. In addition, this approach benefits our business by creating a less parochial culture, as no one person is credited with the success or failure of a particular investment.

Clearly Articulate Investment Risk Parameters

Even when a venture firm has a clear understanding of its business model and investment process, investment risk criteria are often inconsistently applied at the time when a new deal is considered. For some early stage venture firms, this may be appropriate since price will be discounted to adjust for risk, but often enthusiasm for a deal can overshadow a serious flaw in the business. In some investing models, such as ours, it is very important to be consistent. It is our job to effectively map a company against clearly defined risk parameters.

We look for companies that have the potential to be disruptive in their respective markets. In all of our initial investments, we have a cash-on-cash return objective of at least five times our investment. Since we have the benefit of looking at a company that is past the pure start-up stage, we recognize that we must pay a stepped-up valuation for quality companies, but we are also investing with the benefit of more information available. Our goal is to build a portfolio of companies that will produce significantly more winners than losers. This is central to our model to make money for our limited partners.

To ensure that we maintain the proper discipline, we have defined a very clear set of risk criteria that are core to our venture evaluation process. Internally, we refer to this as a company's Risk Adjusted Profile, or RAP Sheet. Our RAP Sheet consists of the following six items:

- Business Model Risk – Often a venture will change or adjust its business model from the original plan as it assesses the market and competition. This speaks to the agility of early stage companies, but can also affect a company's capital requirements, the size of the market opportunity, the profit potential, and the ultimate returns. We do not invest unless the company's business model is "fully baked."

- Capital Structure Risk – We only invest in companies that have "clean" capital structures and have been very capital efficient relative to expected exit values. We don't invest in down rounds, re-starts, or companies with a history of financings with complex terms. The interests of all shareholders should be clearly aligned in the capital structures of companies we consider.

- Customer Acceptance Risk – It is very difficult to understand the customer's appetite for a new venture's products early in its market entry. Often "false positives" can occur where an experienced CEO secures customers more related to a prior relationship than to true market demand. The rate of product adoption can be difficult to estimate. Strong evidence of potential customer traction is a key investment parameter in our risk assessment.

- Market Dynamic Risk – We look very carefully at a market and its dynamics before investing, considering market size, segment growth, and a host of other factors. We evaluate the behavior of the incumbents and look at the quality of emerging players. We also do a formal study of the company's Asia market opportunity to augment our analysis. Overall, the timing of a market's evolution becomes a very important criterion in our risk assessment process.

- Technology Risk – Since we are not true seed or start-up stage investors, we are not oriented toward taking technology risk, yet technology differentiation, as the company's basis for a sustainable competitive advantage in the market, is a very important element in our evaluation of an investment opportunity. We therefore will not invest in a company where there is still a risk of failure based on technology issues, but will invest, even at a full valuation, in companies with technology that can be disruptive to their market.

- Venture Management Risk – Obviously, the quality of the management team is critical to the success of any venture. At our stage of investing, a great deal of work has usually gone into putting together a world-class team, by world-class investors, since we require that top-tier venture capitalists, whom we know well, have preceded us in sponsoring the effort. In our risk assessment, we need to be comfortable with the quality of the CEO, the team, and the Board of Directors. We do not invest in "broken" teams or Boards, and we go out of our way to be sure that all the constituents view the company's challenges in the same way.

As investors, we must be intellectually honest in evaluating the downside as well as the upside of a deal. If an opportunity can potentially offer a terrific return, but with risks that are out of line with our investment criteria, we simply pass. Clarity in articulating our risk parameters allows us to quickly screen out deals that do not fit our model, and to focus on those situations that seem to make more sense for us. Also, as an investment team, the closer we adhere to our process and criteria, the more it becomes ingrained in our organization and understood by our partners in the venture community.

The Role of a Managing General Partner

The role of a venture firm's managing general partner involves, in part, the organization's administrative aspects, ranging from reviewing quarterly financial statements to spearheading fundraising activities. But in my mind, the most important role of the managing partner is much more about empowering the investment team and fostering a shared sense of company values.

To empower the investment team, the managing general partner must be a guardian of the investment decision process to ensure that all investment professionals are respected and heard. In our firm, every investment decision requires an opinion by every investment professional. This forces us all to do sufficient independent work on each deal to be confident of a defensible point of view. Given our stage focus, it is particularly important for us to be reality-based in our thinking. Unlike some firms where a managing or senior partner can approve or block a deal, we believe that true integrity in the process of making investment decisions will lead to a greater focus on all the facts, and place a premium on seeking the best answers to the most difficult questions. Also, the conscious decision to have deals approved by a majority of the investment team, as opposed to a unanimous vote, allows for a process that encourages a dissenting voice, even from a junior professional.

The managing general partner can also influence how the team spends its time. In the venture business, we make many choices each day to allocate time to things that all seem legitimate and productive, but are not necessarily optimal to the firm's overall performance. At JAFCO, we look at our firm foremost as a business. We view ourselves less as a platform for dealmakers and more as an investment business, building and managing a balanced portfolio of successful investments. An investment team that thinks this way often prioritizes its activities differently. As an example, we can look at the deals in our queue each week and choose to focus our collective time on the one deal that appears most promising, regardless of who sourced the deal or how it came to us. We can then, as a team, concentrate on evaluating the company and if appropriate, pursue winning the deal with a single-minded focus.

These aspects of the managing general partner's role protect a shared sense of goals, empowerment, mutual respect, and collaboration. With that, a venture firm is well served by further developing its core values and investment philosophies.

Build a Common Set of Core Values and Investing Philosophies

At an off-site meeting, venture capitalists typically reflect on their core values and investment philosophies. This important exercise should be re-visited on a regular basis. Even venture firms that stylistically are composed of individual contributors benefit from a common set of values and beliefs.

At JAFCO Ventures we are very proud of our core values and investment philosophies and in fact publish them directly on our Web site.

"Though our capital is new and our thinking is fresh, our investment philosophy more closely resembles the traditions of the venture capital business of the past. Our beliefs are reflected in the following tenets:

- Venture capital investing is a service business.
- We strongly believe in the value of partnering and relationships.
- Excellence in our value-added propositions is core to our business.

- The value-creation process works best when there is alignment of interest among all constituents.
- We are unwavering with respect to our ethical compass heading.

Our view of the world is very simple. Portfolio companies are our clients. Colleagues that are top-tier venture capital investors are our customers. Limited partners are our shareholders. We firmly believe that managing a modest-sized fund is fundamental to optimal performance for all of these constituents."

Core values are not just a bunch of "touchy-feely" words. They matter a great deal in any organization and especially in a business where you are entrusted with other people's money. A common set of core values and investment philosophies will foster a predictable response from any member of a team in a given situation. It develops a common set of behavior among individuals with different backgrounds and skills. Through these values, a venture firm develops a sense of its personality and develops a reputation that transcends individual contributors.

It's More about Art than Science

Even though as venture capitalists we typically invest in leading-edge technology companies, our business is more about art than science. Developing an intuitive sense for a company's likely success can be more important than evaluating objective data. Yet one must also be grounded in reality, or emotion can lead to a bad investment decision. The dynamic of getting into deals, leading syndicates, or "having a seat at the table" can be more related to understanding human nature than possessing great technical skills. These are among the many reasons that venture capital is an apprentice business where experience matters and great judgment is highly valued.

In the venture business, making money for your limited partners comes down to adhering to the following basic ideas:

- Of all of the decisions that you make in the venture capital business, from evaluating a technology to helping to select the right CEO, no decision is more important than your first decision to invest in a company. If you get this right, the path may not be easy, but at least you have a chance of success. If you get this decision wrong, the path will require even more work, be much more painful, and result in scant rewards, if any.

- The price you pay for a deal matters a lot. It is easy to lose valuation discipline, particularly when competing to invest in a company. Do not convince yourself that attractive terms justify a high valuation. It is also tempting to overpay for high profile companies, but these don't always translate into great hits. Even when they do, the returns still must be consistent with your business model or the opportunity cost in dollars and effort will affect overall fund performance.

- The importance of determining the right timing and price at which to exit an investment should not be underestimated. Optimizing exit values requires an assessment of present versus future values, but it is also about balancing reality versus perception. Some exits are obvious. But often, for truly interesting companies with billion-dollar market capitalization potential, it can be difficult to know what to do when an attractive suitor appears at your doorstep. Many companies (and investors) are glad they said "no," and many wish they hadn't.

Will It Be Back to the Future or a Brave New World?

Will the venture capital business go back to the future or enter a brave new world? In my view it will be both. I believe that over time, the internal style and values of venture firms will increasingly return to the past, with smaller fund sizes and more of a team-based approach to investment decisions. I also think that we will see the re-emergence of venture investors that think more like the generalists of the past rather than pure domain experts focused only on a particular sub-sector of technology. A balance of vision, agility, and discipline will continue to be important, and experience, as always, will matter immensely. I also believe that among the better venture firms, the bar will be set very high for sponsoring a new venture, recognizing the time and effort it takes to build a great company.

In contrast, although I predict that venture firms will operate internally more as they did in the past, externally, we are entering a brave new world. We are seeing the emergence of a new set of rules for the venture business. The bursting of the Internet bubble set back the markets for purchasing technology products, and severely damaged the credibility of venture-backed companies with U.S. customers. Fortunately, with the globalization of technology markets, newly formed ventures today have more options to consider and are able to think differently. The world is shrinking and companies are focusing earlier on global market opportunities and resources. With highly educated, less expensive offshore labor and appropriate communications, start-up ventures can reduce the cost of building and supporting new products. The sales and marketing plans of new ventures typically incorporate thinking about global markets much earlier in their evolution.

For example, Asia has become a prime focus because, as a whole, it represents the largest and fastest growing market for technology products in the world. Early stage technology companies also benefit from the tendency of customers in Asia to evaluate products based upon specifications and objective performance measures versus an emphasis on brand value alone. Many of these customers are willing to do business with relatively young companies if they can be properly validated by strong U.S. backers and marquee customers. For early stage companies with differentiated technology, this affords a significant opportunity to build large revenue streams early in their evolution.

In many ways, although it is unclear how globalization will ultimately evolve, it has become a very important issue today. Since the venture capital business embraces change more as an opportunity than a threat, one can only imagine the exciting times that lie ahead.

Concluding Thoughts

Thus far, my journey in venture capital has certainly never been dull. The highs are exhilarating and the lows devastating. I feel very blessed to have been a part of the venture industry for a long time. It is a business based on a system of symbiotic relationships where we grow through a state of perpetual learning and teaching. The opportunity to help great entrepreneurs is as exciting to me as ever. It is also very energizing to be part of a world that provides such a remarkable window into the future.

I have always believed that success in life is predicated upon a balance between action and patience. In a similar way, success in the venture business requires a balance between passion and opportunity, for all of the conviction in the world cannot overcome a market that is not ready to embrace a new idea.

What is most exciting to me about the venture capital business today, as in the past, is that it is fundamentally about change. Through good times and bad, the element of change always paves the way to do something new. Some will confuse the art of venture capital with just plain luck. Others will take disproportionate credit for a success based upon their skill and daring. In my view, good fortune does play a role in the outcome, but as Louis Pasteur once said, "Chance favors the prepared mind."

Born in New York City, Joe Horowitz studied engineering at Columbia University's School of Engineering and Applied Sciences, where he was a Sloan Scholar, and subsequently transferred to Columbia College where he earned his bachelor's degree in Economics (A.B. 1973). He then spent four years in various management roles at the University of California Medical Center in San Francisco and other major health care institutions in the United States and Europe before attending The Wharton Graduate School of Business (M.B.A. 1979). He first entered the venture capital business in the late 1970s, when he joined Exxon Enterprises, the venture capital arm of Exxon Corporation.

In the early 1980s, when venture capital partnerships began to expand, Mr. Horowitz moved back to California to join the newly formed U.S. Venture Partners (USVP) in Menlo Park. He became USVP's first associate and fourth investment professional. The first deal that he worked on was the seed financing of Sun Microsystems in the spring of 1982. After thirteen months, Mr. Horowitz became a general partner of the firm and subsequently a member of U.S. Venture Partner's Executive Committee. In addition to Sun, over the course of his ten-year involvement at USVP, the firm backed over one hundred start-up companies. In addition to his activities as a venture capital investor, Mr. Horowitz took on various operational and fund raising responsibilities for USVP, and in 1990 led an extensive effort to restructure the firm. He also served as a director of the Western Association of Venture Capitalists.

In 1992, Mr. Horowitz left USVP, and with the support of Bessemer Venture Partners, Benchmark Capital, and Institutional Venture Partners (IVP) developed a very successful venture advisory business. This allowed him to work more deeply with venture opportunities as an independent advisor and Board member. Over six years, he actively assisted client ventures on strategic issues, financing challenges, management team needs, and merger negotiations. He consummated numerous financings with top-tier venture capital firms and corporate strategic partners.

Furthering his interest in the entrepreneurial process, in 1998 Mr. Horowitz became chairman and CEO of Geocast Network Systems, an ambitious start-up company whose initial investors included the Mayfield Fund, Kleiner Perkins Caufield & Byers, and IVP. Despite a world-class team, extraordinary corporate partners, and some early commercial success, the company failed after the Internet bubble burst to the disappointment of the shareholders and Mr. Horowitz personally.

With the technology markets in decline, Mr. Horowitz took some time off to pursue personal interests and enjoy more time with his family. After considering a number of opportunities, he decided to come full circle and formally reenter the venture capital business, believing that it would be an excellent time to invest in new ideas as the technology market gained in strength.

In June of 2003, Mr. Horowitz joined JAFCO Ventures as the firm's managing general partner. JAFCO Ventures, a long-standing venture capital franchise, is the domestic affiliate of Tokyo-based JAFCO Co. Ltd, the largest venture capital firm in Japan with funds under management in many parts of Asia, including China. When the JAFCO domestic investment team spun out to form a new firm in late 2002, JAFCO re-launched its U.S. venture capital activities with a new $100 million fund.

In his reentry into the venture capital business, Mr. Horowitz had a mandate to design a venture capital business model capable of delivering superior returns based upon JAFCO's strategic value, his extensive venture experience, and the opportunity to look at the deal flow from top-tier venture capital investors—an interesting platform from which to provide a view of the venture capital business today.

Keys to Success in Venture Capital

Howard M. Anderson

Senior Managing Director & Founder
YankeeTek Ventures

Achieving Success

Success in venture capitalism starts with spotting great opportunities for investment. Finding the right companies to invest in is the key to success. Unfortunately, spotting those companies is not easy. There's no formula. What I generally do is to take some macro trends that I think are going to hit and invest in them. In the year 2000, I did that with open source software. By the time everybody understood that it was an opportunity, it was too late for them. Once an investment choice is made, success is determined by the size of the return. Personally, I love it if my companies go public. My second favorite outcome is when we merge companies. The best result is a public offering, and then we may sell the company. Second best is selling it for a high price.

Successful venture capitalists generally come from two different backgrounds. Both sets have run companies in the past, but some have done it on the financial side and some on the operations side. There are positives and negatives to both. The financial side does beautiful models, but it doesn't necessarily breed judgment. The operations side is not as much into models, but they have experience running a company, and they probably have experience in picking management teams. Both sides probably have made a few mistakes, and hope they'll make fewer of them as they move forward.

It's also important to stay on top of industry knowledge and keep up-to-date with the latest trends and developments. Toward that end, I buy a lot of dumb people a lot of overpriced lunches. I attend any number of industry meetings each year. I read dozens of periodicals. I listen to my students and I'm always learning things. In spite of all my efforts, I'm always worried that I might miss that next trend.

The Role of the Venture Capitalist

Venture capitalists have three main functions. One, we invest other people's money into companies. Two, we figure out how to help companies build strategic alliances with customers. Three, we fire management when they're not doing their job and we help recruit new management.

When we invest other people's money, we take money from universities and pension funds and put it into a common pool. Then we find the companies that we think are going to succeed and we invest that money in those companies. In our case, that is the job of the three partners inside the venture firm. In determining how to invest that money, we ask questions like, is the technology unique? Does the firm have intellectual property that is its own? Is it defendable? Can we find a market that is growing and large, and can we find that this technology can be ten times faster, ten times cheaper or ten times more cost effective? If we find all of these to be true, we consider investing.

Building strategic alliances for companies is also a big part of a venture capitalist's role. Let's say I have a company with good technology that might be important to building a better battery. I might introduce them to someone like Black and Decker, who makes cordless drills. That battery might be able to allow them to recharge a dead cordless drill in fifteen minutes, not two and a half hours. Over the years, we have built relationships with nearly all of the Fortune 500 companies. We know exactly who to call and they know we're not going to waste their time.

When management has to be fired, it is usually done by the partner who is on the board of directors. Sometimes, management is fired because the job has grown. Sometimes the founder has taken it as far as they can go, and they need help. Sometimes it means that the CEO has to step down to become a valued employee and sometimes they leave the company. It is the role of the board of directors to do the actual firing, but we sit on the board. Recruiting new management is also our job; as board members, we are responsible for interviewing candidates. We try to take people we know in the industry and convince them that they want to take this job.

Rules for Venture Capital

I have a few general rules for investing venture capital. You should make sure to find a real market that's growing, find intellectual property, and be careful that you're not in the firing range of a big company that may roll over your company by accident. For example, you should be wary of investing in a product that's just a feature. Before you know it, Microsoft might give it away for free in its next release. Microsoft didn't try to pick on your company, but your company still got killed. In that situation, you should have known better.

There are also some specific rules that I've developed by learning from past mistakes. For example, I do not like to invest in husband and wife teams, for several reasons. A) They may vote together on every issue, when you'd like to see some independent thinking. B) They often get divorced, and that divorce tends to play out in the boardroom. C) If I lose one, I may lose the other, and they both might be valuable.

Another specific rule is that I don't like to invest in companies where research is in one location and marketing is in another location. That never seems to work, because they just send e-mails back and forth to each other, blaming all the problems on the other side. The marketing guy says, "This is a product the market doesn't want." The engineers say, "Well, this is the product you told me you wanted six months ago." Products change, and I need the interchange—both formal and informal—between whole parts of the company. When you don't have that, the product usually will fail.

Entrepreneurial Mistakes

The life of a venture capitalist involves myriad interactions with entrepreneurs. I've learned that there are a few common mistakes and misperceptions held by entrepreneurs. First, entrepreneurs should understand what it is that venture capitalists do. Venture capitalists are not angel investors. An angel investor puts the money in and gives advice. Once a venture capitalist puts their money in, they are going to be controlling and vocal. They are going to spend time with a company, and if the CEO and his team do not perform, they will be replaced. That's something that entrepreneurs have to understand. If they come in with rosy projections, they will be held accountable to those projections.

Another common mistake that entrepreneurs make is to hold on to a Pollyanna's belief that technology alone will lead to markets. That rarely happens. Also, entrepreneurs often fail to recognize how quickly, or slowly, things happen. Their time horizons are sometimes woefully optimistic. It takes time for almost everything: time to develop the product, time to test the product, time to get the first customer, time to revise the product, time to build distribution, time to build repair and maintenance. All of these seem to take longer than many entrepreneurs anticipate.

Entrepreneurial Shortcomings

In addition to common mistakes, entrepreneurs also seem to share a set of shortcomings. The most common problem is working with entrepreneurs who are too visionary or not visionary enough. The second is entrepreneurs who may not have the people skills or the experience to take their company to the next level. The third situation is that the market may have changed on the entrepreneurs. They may not recognize the change or know what they need to do about it.

If an entrepreneur is too visionary, he may not have a good understanding of how long his cash will last. He might be trying to build a product a generation or two away, when a simpler product that serves an immediate need might be more receptive in the market. You need a visionary on some things, but you need a solid operations implementer on others. Small companies don't have the luxury of excess management. They usually are thin in management, and that's why sometimes changes need to be made.

On the other hand, if an entrepreneur is not visionary enough, they may be too short-sighted. For example, an entrepreneur taking on a consulting project might not get the product done in time because they're trying to get the project to profitability too soon. Our view is that if they were more visionary, they would realize that they could stand the loss if the product gets to market sooner, and they shouldn't subjugate the potential of the company for short-term profits or cash.

In either case, as a venture capitalist, you would first try to coach and explain. Then you would probably try to help augment management. After that, sometimes you have to try to change management. It's just like being a parent. You don't take Draconian measures at first, but when you've reached the conclusion that the management isn't going to get the company to where it has to be, you can't be afraid to make changes.

Sometimes the entrepreneur doesn't have the right people skills or experience. In that event, the baton has to get passed to new management.

It's not a question of being bad guys or good guys. In the end, our bias has to be toward building a company. We can't wait for management to mature or acquire people skills, so we have to bring in more professional and experienced management. The entrepreneur might be fine to get the company to one level, but taking it to the next level may require a different team.

When the situation is a change in the market, it's difficult for venture capital to deal with. Sometimes it's hard to tell exactly when the market is changing. It might give you signals by buying slower or buying a different product, or the things that made the market look advantageous at first may look less advantageous. For example, the product may be appropriate for security, but it may require massive changes on the part of the customers. We may come to the conclusion that the product is now nice to have, but not something customers have to have. The product may need to be re-tasked to a different market, and often a company can't afford to go after two markets simultaneously. Changing markets is difficult for a company because they may need more money. They may have to change the product or they may have to change the distribution. They may have to change almost everything in the hope of surviving and finding a market that wants their product.

In this situation, the first step is to try to use logic. Then use examples of other companies that have made this change. If that doesn't work, at long last you use your power as a board member. Often the venture capitalists as a group will compel the board to say we've got to change and we've got to change now. Sometimes management is in denial that the market is really changed. They may think it is a temporary dip. They may feel that the market will come back to them, but often it will not.

Venture Capital Mistakes

Entrepreneurs are not the only ones who make mistakes—venture capitalists make them as well. Venture capitalists make all the same mistakes that entrepreneurs make; for example, they misjudge the degree of difficulty in getting customers or companies to change their behavior because of something new. That takes a lot of time. Another mistake that venture capitalists make is to believe the entrepreneur. They underestimate the amount of capital it takes. A good CEO of a company makes sure his company doesn't run out of money. He's got to understand his company shouldn't run out of money. He doesn't want to take so much money that he dilutes ownership, but not too little that he starves his company. And that's a mistake we also make in venture capital.

Another mistake venture capitalists make is to underestimate the difficulty in achieving the technology. Sometimes we go into a situation and we're not sure exactly what the resources are that the company is going to need. So it may be that it's beyond the technical capabilities of the firm that we've invested in. It may be beyond the state of the art. It may be beyond the state of the people that we've brought in. It may be that it requires a much more massive investment than we anticipated. These are all mistakes we make.

The Management Team

To overcome shortcomings on the entrepreneurial and venture capital sides, I try to put the best possible management team together. I look for experienced people who have performed well in the past and successfully run profit centers. I also look for a high-energy level. To combine experience with energy level, I look for people in their thirties and forties, not in their twenties and fifties. In their twenties, people have more energy but not enough experience. In their fifties, people have a lot of experience but not enough energy. After looking at age, I look at what they've done, and I believe that gives me my best indication as to how well they're going to perform. Past experience is the best predictor of future experience.

The role of a board member on a venture firm is intensive. We talk or visit with our companies on a weekly basis. The board meetings are monthly. These are productive meetings—not just a time to pass information along. The board really does run the company at the early venture capital stage.

We work with the entire management team, which includes people like the CFO and CTO. At the time that we work with companies, the CFO is really less important. They may have the title CFO, but we don't need a Chief Financial Officer until about a year before the company goes public.

Up until that point, a company raises money one year at a time. They may need somebody to run the books, but the CFO is of lesser importance.

The CTO, on the other hand, is of high importance because he's the one in whom we're really investing. In that position, we've got to have someone who has run engineering teams, knows development cycles, knows how long things take, and can recruit first-rate technical people and keep them. In our case, investor relations are not important. That is because we're investing in private companies. Investor relations only get to be important once the company has filed for an IPO.

Stages of Company Development

We divide companies up into four different stages. The first stage is the seed stage, where the company may have an idea and they have a sparse, incomplete management team. The second stage is the early stage. The company may have a product that is close to being completed, but is not yet complete. The third stage is the mezzanine stage. The company has got a product, they're in the market, and they're making sales, but they may be unprofitable. The fourth stage is called late stage. This would be right before a company goes public. They've got a product, they've got a team, and they've got acceleration. They're growing and there's acceptance in the market for their product, although they may not be profitable at this point. But they're certainly growing.

Of those stages, we generally invest in early stage companies. That means that we don't invest in profitable companies. There are good venture capital firms out there that only invest in companies that are profitable. It's a different risk portfolio. Their downside risk is much less than ours. Their upside is usually less than ours, but they still perform well.

When companies are primarily doing international business, it's a more difficult thing for us to assess. That is because the due diligence process takes longer. We like to see a technology company get 30 to 40 percent of its sales internationally. That shows broad support and growth in international markets. It means that I can take the same R&D dollars and divide them among the world's market, not just the U.S. market. If they have an international market and the market is growing, that's an impressive achievement.

A down economy can be a factor, but we expect down economies. No tree grows to the skies. We expect a company to be able to perform in both a down and an up economy. If their product is valuable enough and their sales team is smart enough, they should know how to sell in both a down and an up economy. We understand that a down economy makes it a little bit harder. Investment dollars are harder to get. The customers may wait longer in their decision process. But just because it's a down economy, we don't expect a company to stop its progress.

Factors Affecting Valuations

Valuation is a step-by-step process. First of all, you look for comparables. You look for what other venture investors have invested in similar firms in the recent period, and at what price. For example, a company may be valued at two times next year's sales. If the company projects profitability three years out, what are the public companies comparable to that one? After looking at comparable companies, you take that number and perhaps reduce it because it's still a year or two away.

To demonstrate what kinds of companies would interest me, I'll provide a few hypothetical examples. Let's say a company was at a seed stage, with only an idea and a solid management team in place. I would probably value that idea at somewhere worth $2 and $5 million. I like to get single digits. A management team gives me a reason that it might be worth $4 or $5 million. I am going to assume that I am going to put $5 million into this company, knowing no more than the idea and the management team. That means that the venture group—which may be just me—would own half the company.

A company with about $5 million in sales that loses about $1 million each year would be valued based on different factors. If we're assuming that it's growing at 20 percent a year, which means that there's a chance that within a year or so it would be profitable, I might value this company on the high side at $10 million.

A software company that has $20 million in sales and makes a profit of $2 million a year is a company that is probably worth $15 or $20 million. It might be worth more—as much as $40 million. If they're doing $20 million a year and they're taking $2 million to the bottom line, that's 10 percent. That's pretty good. A company like this would probably be worth fifteen times earnings, which gets me to $30 million.

On the other hand, a biotech company with zero dollars in sales that loses $10 million a year is definitely not the kind of company I would consider investing in. I would run from this company for three reasons. One, I don't have any unfair advantage in biotech and I do in other areas. Two, I don't understand it, and other people do. Three, if this industry is losing so much money, the big pharma companies may want to participate. Also, I may need FDA approval for its products and it is not certain how long that takes. So biotech is not an area that I invest in.

Another company that I would not consider investing in is a company with $100 million in sales, $3 million in profit, three rounds of funding, and plans to go public in a year or so. That company is probably worth $100 million, just because they'd be worth at least one million multiplied by sales. It may be worth more than that, but I'm not going to participate in a round like that. That's a late stage deal. It's not my sweet spot.

Evaluating Growth Potential and Risk

Evaluating a company's growth potential is an important part of the firm's decision to invest. If a company is not growing 20 to 50 percent a year, I'm worried. If you've got a $2 million company, they should do $3 million next year. That's a 50 percent growth. I don't invest in companies that are $100 million in sales. They're too big. And if they're not growing, there's something fatally flawed in the company. I'm not so arrogant that I think I can fix it just because I'm there. So they've got to grow 20 percent minimum per year.

In order to evaluate that potential return, I want to see what they've already done. Where is the product? What's the size of the market? What's their distribution? How are they going to attack the market? Who is their competition? How has their competition grown? Is it a sector that's kind of tired, or is it a whole sector that's growing? I like sectors that grow. If the sector grows, and the company does okay, I should do fine. If they're the best performing company in the sector, but the sector is buggy-whips and it's not growing at all, I might not be able to get anywhere with it.

Another factor in evaluating risks is exit strategies. I have to know when I'm going to get out and how I'm going to get out. I'm not in there forever. I am more of a three to five-year investor, not a long-term investor.

Howard Anderson founded The Yankee Group, a technology research and consulting firm, where he served as president and CEO from 1970 until 2000. The Yankee Group was ultimately acquired by Reuters, a New York Stock Exchange company. Additionally, Mr. Anderson was a co-founder of Battery Ventures, a Boston-based private equity firm specializing in technology companies. He has served as a managing partner and a special limited partner since the company's inception.

Mr. Anderson was recently selected by Network World as one of the 25 most important people in communications. He has presented keynote addresses at both COMDEX and NetWorld+Interop. He is also a contributing columnist to Forbes Magazine and Technology Review. Mr. Anderson is the William Porter Distinguished Lecturer at MIT, where he teaches a course in the management of high technology firms. He received his M.B.A. from Harvard and his B.A. in economics from the University of Pennsylvania.

Legal Issues in Raising Venture Capital: An Overview for Entrepreneurs

Gary L. Benton

Partner

Pillsbury Winthrop Shaw Pittman LLP

Legal Planning in the Venture Fundraising Process

There are three fundamentals required for an emerging growth company to raise venture capital funding: an innovative technology, a solid business plan, and a strong management team. Good legal planning is not a fundamental requirement. A company may have proper corporate structuring, appropriate IP protections, and well-written contracts with its employees, but such legal planning will never be reason enough for a venture investor to fund a company.

On the other hand, countless numbers of startups have failed to raise financing because they did not give appropriate consideration to such legal concerns. If a management team hasn't satisfied certain basic corporate compliance, protection, and planning requirements by the time it seeks funding, it is sending a signal to potential investors that it may not have what it takes to put together a well-rounded business plan.

Legal Steps to Be Taken Prior to Fundraising

Successful companies have corporate structuring designed for venture investment, intellectual property protections for technology, and think strategically about business agreements. A good management team will invest both time and seed capital to work with a lawyer to properly set up a corporation, protect IP and document agreements, and comply with securities laws before trying to raise outside financing.

Proper attention to emerging company legal issues requires the advice of an experienced lawyer who can address the particular goals, requirements, and capabilities of the company and its founders. A corporate structure must be crafted to address the specific goals of the founders, the skill set of the management team, the company's business plan, the particular market space, the current business cycle, and recent changes to the law. These are considerations that can never be properly addressed by copying legal documents used by another company. Good investors can easily tell when a company is put together without proper legal advice.

Setting up a company without proper legal advice is almost always a mistake. Apart from coming across as unprofessional when presenting to investors, a company acting without a lawyer is more likely to engage in securities law violations, make problematic contractual commitments, and fail to pursue IP protections, all of which will be difficult to correct at a later stage.

Addressing legal considerations properly from the start helps make a company attractive to investors, avoids problems and delays in the due diligence process, and substantially reduces costs. Law firms with practices devoted to emerging company work can provide their clients additional resources such as training programs, access to business advisors, and introductions to professional venture investors.

The Funding Process from a Legal Standpoint: Areas of Concern for CEOs/Entrepreneurs

The key for entrepreneurs in the funding process is to obtain a financing package that makes sense for the company and its founders. There are many variables to be considered.

Before asking for funding, a company should develop and articulate a clear business and financial plan so that it knows how much funding is needed, as well as what it will do with this funding. The business plan should include corporate, IP, employment, and commercial considerations.

A company should be properly structured *before* entering into the funding process. A company that does not meet corporate requirements from the start will likely end up with a low valuation and considerable cleanup costs. Almost any equity funding will require some restructuring of the company to implement the financing terms. Nonetheless, failure to implement proper structuring when the company is created can create problems that cannot be corrected. The sources for such problems include using improper forms, using documents created by unqualified lawyers, issuing unauthorized stock, acting without board approval, improperly pricing stock, making stock grants that are undocumented or poorly documented, and failing to do securities compliance.

Companies that sell stock or issue options without proper written agreements in place or without appropriate corporate filings and securities compliance are, simply put, asking for disaster. Such companies and their officers and directors are in violation of the securities laws and could face civil and criminal penalties. Additionally, such companies and their officers and directors are more likely to be sued for breach of contract and fraud.

Often, the problems created by failing to do things properly from the beginning can never fully be rectified by lawyers after the fact; it may be impossible for a lawyer to issue a useful opinion letter on the company at any point in the future once this damage has been done. Accordingly, these companies can usually forget about getting venture funding or having acquisitions or IPOs, simply because there is too much risk for new investors or acquirers.

Due Diligence from a Legal Perspective: Looking for Reasons Not to Fund

Due diligence is a legal, accounting, and business review of a company that is conducted prior to an investment being made in a company. The scope of a due diligence review will vary based on the company and the requirements of the investors. Although due diligence review is a task for the investors, a company seeking funding will want to be sure it is in top shape before it presents itself to potential investors.

Investors may rely on outside experts to assist with due diligence. The outcome of the due diligence review is that the investors may require certain steps to be taken before an investment commitment is made. The due diligence may frame certain representations that the investors will require in the financing documents. Another possible conclusion from the due diligence examination is that there may be fundamental problems with the company that will simply cause the investors to walk away from the opportunity.

Legal due diligence breaks down into four broad categories: corporate, IP, employment, and commercial due diligence.

Corporate due diligence includes reviewing the company's charter documents (Articles/Certificate of Incorporation, Bylaws, board resolutions, etc.) to be sure the corporation is properly incorporated and structured itself. The corporate due diligence process involves confirming that required foreign state qualifications are in place, reviewing any initial stock issuances, and reviewing options plans, grants, and other preemptive right grants to be sure they have been structured, priced, and documented properly. Stockholder agreements and investor rights agreements will also be reviewed to confirm they are reasonable and properly implemented.

Corporate due diligence includes ensuring that the company has complied with all federal and state securities laws when issuing stock or options. Legal counsel will verify that issued stock has been fully paid, ledgers are up to date, and properly legended stock certificates have been issued. A company undergoing corporate due diligence will be asked to provide an up-to-date stock capitalization table and to confirm that its board and officers have been counseled on fiduciary duties and other legal obligations.

IP due diligence requires confirming that a company has properly protected its intellectual property through timely patent filings and other procedures. Only a qualified patent lawyer has the skills required to do a proper patent validity and infringement analysis. In addition to patent protection, they should have proper agreements in place to protect copyright ownership. The company should take steps to register trademarks. Necessary Web domains should be reserved, and all officers and employees should sign confidentiality/invention assignment agreements. The company should have procedures in place to protect trade secrets and other confidential information. Likewise, IP counsel should confirm that any assignments of IP are valid and properly documented.

Due diligence regarding employment issues involves reviewing employment and independent contractor protocols and verifying that all officers, employees, and contractors have signed employment, confidentiality, and invention assignment agreements in place. Employee contracts and other documentation will be reviewed to confirm that compensation obligations are reasonable. Counsel doing employment due diligence will also confirm that proper and appropriate documentation, approvals, and vesting provisions are in place for stock and option grants. Employment due diligence also involves confirming that basic employment, payroll, and tax systems and procedures are in place.

Commercial due diligence requires reviewing any key contracts and licenses to be sure they are consistent with the company's corporate documentation, contain accurate company representations, and do not impose any burdensome restraints on the company. Counsel will check to ensure that the company does not have any significant liabilities to the founders, employees, business partners, outside lenders, or others. Contracts and licenses may be reviewed in detail to ensure that the company has not made unreasonable commercial commitments, valuable rights have not been contracted away, and the company will have the flexibility to assign contracts or engage in other desired transactions later.

Commercial due diligence will often verify that there are no threatening or pending legal claims against the company. Investors will also want to be certain that there are no tax liens or judgments that might interfere with the fundraising process or the activities of the company in the future.

Legal Issues Regarding Term Sheets: Setting the Investment Terms between VCs and the Company

A term sheet sets out the basic legal terms of a financing including valuation, liquidation, preferences, and structuring. Term sheets that are sufficiently detailed and prepared carefully will serve as a road map for the stock purchase documents. Term sheets that are poorly drafted will require extended negotiation of the purchase documents and additional legal costs.

Smart entrepreneurs will be guided by their lawyers before they start negotiating terms. Once a term sheet is received from a venture investor, good lawyers will spend considerable time with their clients reviewing the proposed terms.

The company may prepare a proposed term sheet for angel investors or as a basis for negotiations with venture investors. Most venture firms prefer, however, to provide their own term sheets. Venture investors will provide a term sheet when they are prepared to make an investment in a company. Accordingly, receiving a term sheet is a major step in the financing process. Care should be given as to the binding nature of term sheets and whether the company is free to continue to explore other funding options after the term sheet is accepted. It is not unusual for venture investors to include "no-shop" provisions. Venture investors do not want their term sheets shopped around and expect their offers to be kept confidential. Venture investors expect that any issues in written term sheets be addressed promptly.

After the basic terms are negotiated by the company, the final term sheet negotiations should be handled by lawyers for both sides. Once the terms sheet is negotiated, the drafting process begins. Drafting financing documents is a costly process, ranging from $50,000 to $100,000 for the company on a typical deal, and it is inappropriate for either side to change the deal terms absent exceptional circumstances.

Deal Terms – The Top "Deal Stoppers" Between Investors and Companies

To obtain financing, company management must be realistic about deal terms to make the investment worthwhile for the investors. Disagreements over deal terms tend to fall into two broad categories: disagreements over ownership/control of the company and investor discomfort with the business model. The most common "deal stoppers" are as follows:

1. The parties cannot reach agreement on valuation (i.e., the ownership percentages of the investors and the founders) for the company;
2. The parties cannot reach agreement on liquidation preferences (i.e., the payout allocation between the investors and the founders in an acquisition);
3. The parties cannot reach agreement on control issues such as board composition or officer selection;
4. Due diligence discloses a defect in the IP or IP protection;
5. Due diligence discloses a defect in the financial projections.

Valuations for a company can vary considerably, but a financial advisor experienced with venture investment in the company's sector should be able to guide the company on appropriate formulas for valuations and provide reality checks on the financial projections in a business plan. Likewise, lawyers experienced with emerging company venture financing are a good resource on standards for deal terms on investor payouts and controls.

Deal Terms – Areas of Concern for Entrepreneurs

When it comes time to negotiate funding terms, the most critical technical issue is valuation—specifically, how much is the company worth and how much funding will it receive. Valuation determines the percentage of the company the founders must surrender for the investment and the resulting percentage to be owned by the investors.

Pre-money valuation is the valuation of the company prior to investment. Post-money valuation is the valuation of the company after the investment and simply the sum of the pre-money valuation plus the cash being invested into the company in the financing.

A basic principal in venture capital financing is that equity is utilized to attract new investment and in turn, substantially increase share value. The goal is substantial appreciation in share value, not maintenance or growth of ownership percentage. This is a difficult concept for many new entrepreneurs because, understandably, they do not want their ownership interest diluted. Setting a valuation requires finding an acceptable balance between giving up ownership interest (and possibly control) in a company and attracting new investment in the company.

Entrepreneurs should develop a clear sense of what is a reasonable valuation for their company. To answer this question, entrepreneurs need to have an understanding of the company's financial needs, financial potential, the valuations of comparable companies, and the trends in the market.

Early stage companies with good technology concepts but no prototypes, a limited business infrastructure, and no sales history will be valued significantly less than a company that has built a strong IP portfolio around its technology, assembled a proven management team, developed marketing/sales channels, and has an established and growing revenue stream. In essence, a company is not going to have the valuation of Google merely based on the promise of its technology. High valuations come through good ideas, smart planning, and hard work.

Apart from valuation, there are many other important considerations in the fundraising process for entrepreneurs and the company from the legal perspective, including liquidation provisions, conversion, protective provisions, and board representation. The two major considerations are liquidation preferences (i.e., what the investors and the founders will each receive on an acquisition exit for the company) and management structuring (i.e., who will control the board and who will manage the company).

Liquidation provisions and related issues concerning conversion and antidilution protections are complicated terms. The financial consequences of liquidation and conversion require financial modeling by companies and investors so that they may determine their potential returns at different acquisition prices.

Although easier to understand, management structuring also requires considerable planning. Determinations must be made by founders and investors as to who should control the board of directors, what investors and investor groups should be represented on the board of directors, the value in having independent directors, and the methodology in selecting board members. Related issues concern the size of the board and the appointment of observers. Management structuring is further complicated by legal restrictions on the election of board members. Accordingly, structuring goals must often be addressed through private voting agreements between major stockholders. There are other legal restraints and obligations on board members due to legal requirements regarding corporate governance.

Many deal terms, such as registration rights, may be so complicated that negotiation is best left to the lawyers for the company and investors. Entrepreneurs should expect that their personal stockholder interests and employment terms will be addressed in the funding process. Prior to the funding process, entrepreneurs should consider what percentage of their stock should be fully vested and acceptable vesting terms for the balance of their stock. Entrepreneurs should be prepared to discuss their salary requirements, service guarantees, and their willingness to step aside when the company is at a different stage.

Finally, there are many intangible considerations for entrepreneurs when bringing on outside financing; the most important consideration is whether the entrepreneurs are turning to investors with whom they can work well and who have the ability to help you grow the company. In many cases, it is worth forgoing a higher valuation in return for working with a venture investor who can help the entrepreneur build the company.

Strategies That May Haunt Entrepreneurs Down the Road

There are thousands of ways an entrepreneur can go wrong with a company. A company with great technology will go nowhere if the company does not have a sound business plan and legal structure. Likewise, an experienced and cohesive management team will fail if the technology it develops does not have proper legal protections.

Founders should obtain experienced legal advice before making promises to issue stock or options. Every stock offer and issuance, including issuances to the founders themselves, is subject to the securities laws. There are many technical issues involved in a stock issuance. Problems often arise when the correct approvals and filings have not been made, when the stock price is not appropriate, or when there is no securities law compliance.

Many mistakes are made in negotiating financing terms. Some of the mistakes are technical errors. Others are strategic errors. The most common problems are traced to entrepreneurs who make agreements without understanding deal terms and the practical implications of their investment agreements. Too often investors think the negotiations are over after an agreement is made as to valuation and investment amount. In reality, the deal is in the small print.

Not surprisingly, the biggest mistake entrepreneurs make is giving too much to an investor who is not trustworthy. Entrepreneurs who don't rely on legal counsel can give away their companies and not even know it.

Another big mistake entrepreneurs make is not trusting an investor who can help the company. Entrepreneurs who won't rely on others who can help them are throwing their companies away and don't even know it.

It is very difficult to balance and identify these issues of trustworthiness. Founders are always fearful of losing control—a reasonable concern—while at the same time, there are some founders who refuse to recognize the limits of their capabilities; they turn away quality investors (and other advisors) who can help take the company to the next level.

Good investors provide more than cash—they provide leads on later funding rounds, introductions to strategic partners, and management support. Founders need to recognize the funding process is not about getting cash and minimizing dilution of their ownership percentage. It is about developing the best strategy to commercialize a new technology. That goal is best served when founders agree to reasonable controls (including vesting provisions, voting agreements, and an independent board) and welcome support from their investors and advisors.

Legal Areas of Concern for Venture Investors

Venture investment is a business; it promotes the advancement of new technologies only if there is money to be made in doing so. The key for VCs in the investment process is to make an investment that can maximize return and minimize risk. VCs need to provide strong rates of return to their investors and having the right legal terms is a critical part of that process.

From that perspective, important considerations include: valuation, vesting, liquidation, conversion, anti-dilution protections, protective provisions, and board representation. Investors may want to consider milestone payments, in which case they should be sure they have participation rights and controls over future rounds of financing or other major corporate transactions. Investors will also want to be sure they have appropriate information rights, registration rights, and co-sale protections.

Although valuation is the most significant issue for both entrepreneurs and VCs to consider, there are many other issues that will fundamentally affect the company and its investors. Other major issues to consider include: liquidation benefits (i.e., what an investor will receive compared to the founders on an M&A exit); protective rights (i.e., what veto power the investors have over major decisions, such as new financings, acquisitions, and expenses); and management strategy, such as who will be on the board and who will be running the company (i.e., how the investors and founders will work together).

Of course, every venture investor has his or her own investing style and strategy. With respect to negotiating legal terms, some VCs focus more on protecting the downside with milestone payments, redemption rights, ratchet clauses, and numerous protective provisions; others focus more on the upside with high valuations, liquidations multiples, uncapped participation rights, and preemptive rights. Smart venture investors find a balance. They rely on simple standard terms that provide protections while at the same time giving their portfolio companies room to grow.

Ultimately, what works best is a legal structure that allows management to do its job and provides the investor a role in supporting the growth of the company.

Other Legal Agreements between VC and the Company

A financing package will contain a number of legal documents. In addition to stock purchase agreements, venture investors will almost always require founders to agree to stock vesting provisions. Vesting provisions require founders to remain employed with the company for a period of years in order to receive their full ownership percentage of the stock. Likewise, investors will typically insist that all employees sign confidentiality/invention assignment agreements.

It is typical to have voting agreements or shareholder agreements in place, principally to control allocation of board seats. Likewise, it is typical to have investor rights agreements, which address access to company information, registration rights, and various transfer restrictions.

International Venture Deals

International venture deals involve all the issues involved in a domestic deal along with an entire new set of challenges. International deals involve parties from different cultures with diverse business and legal expectations.

Technically, international deals involve multiple sets of laws and complicated issues over applicable laws. To be done properly, international deals require special corporate structuring, often in offshore jurisdictions, to create companies that can go public and provide appropriate tax benefits.

In an international deal, IP must be protected in multiple jurisdictions. Contract and employment issues will also involve multijurisdictional considerations. Many venture investors already require foreign outsourcing to be a necessary component of business plans. Finally, special attention must be paid to dispute resolution mechanisms because U.S. Court judgments will not be enforced by most foreign countries.

As technology and economies outside the U.S. develop, we will see a growing number of international technology deals coming from China, India, Israel, and other locations. We will see more companies incorporating in foreign jurisdictions, such as the Caymans and Bermuda. We will also see companies offshoring their operations to Eastern Europe, India, China, and elsewhere in Asia. Many new technology companies will go public on the stock markets in London, Hong Kong, Shanghai, Tokyo, and Singapore. Expertise in cross-border technology investment will be critical to handle all of these transactions.

Conclusions

Proper legal planning is a critical component of the venture investment process. Companies that address corporate, intellectual property, and employment/commercial legal issues up front will have a higher likelihood of obtaining venture funding and growing into successful companies. There are practical, fundamental, and strategic legal considerations to be made at every step of the venture funding process. A company that invests the resources to rely on quality legal counsel and other appropriate advisors will have the best chance for success.

Gary L. Benton is a partner in the Palo Alto office of the international law firm Pillsbury Winthrop Shaw Pittman LLP. Mr. Benton advises a broad array of U.S. and international technology companies, telecommunication companies and venture investors on corporate, commercial, and intellectual property law issues, including corporate formation, venture capital financing, corporate governance, contracts, licensing, joint ventures, M&A, U.S., and offshore listings, and other strategic U.S. and international business law matters. He is qualified to practice law as both a U.S lawyer and an English solicitor.

Essential Components for Investing in Venture Capital

John Higginbotham

Founder & Chairman
SpaceVest

The Keys to Success

There's no more fulfilling a feeling than helping people be successful. Venture capital is incredibly exciting and rewarding work—taking a young situation with a lot of promise and turning it into something successful.

The key characteristics that make a successful venture capitalist are realism, pragmatism, common sense, and confidence. One must ultimately trust one's own judgment. This is not arrogance or ego, as arrogance and ego have gotten plenty of people in trouble. It also takes a touch of insanity, and I'm not joking. In some ways, if one really knew what it took to be successful in this business before getting into it, one probably would not choose it for a profession. A lot of sleepless nights and heavy lifting go into making a deal work.

Venture capital is not a business for everyone. It takes confidence and a willingness to make a decision without fear of failure or rejection. Analytical skills and interpersonal skills are also a big part of it. In my judgment, it takes special talent to be a successful venture capitalist, and quite frankly, some luck. Any successful venture capitalist that tells you there isn't some luck involved is kidding you.

Persistence and commitment are also important. A venture capitalist signs up for a partnership that goes on for at least ten years. It's a long-term career commitment. Having integrity and honesty goes without saying, because a VC is a fiduciary for people's money. A sense of responsibility is also crucial, and a sense of greed—you've got to know when to take advantage of the opportunity.

There are really two types of venture capitalists out there: builders and traders. The traders are transaction oriented and the builders are oriented toward building a company. In my judgment, the builders are the classic venture capitalists. They are the ones who are really stepping back and approaching the investment decision in the context of what it takes to build a successful business for the long term. And ultimately that's where the greatest returns will come.

Doing Deals

As a venture capitalist, there are two primary functions: raising money and doing deals. Doing deals includes the sourcing, the diligence, the negotiations of the deal, post-investment management, and ultimately organizing an exit.

Deal sourcing is identifying and finding investment opportunities. There are many activities involved, everything from tracking markets, going to venture fairs, and networking with other venture groups, strategic players, entrepreneurs, investment bankers, and any number of other sources. There are a lot of different sources for deals and you've got to work the network in those various venues to find opportunities.

If you find a deal that appears interesting through the sourcing process, the next step is the diligence activity. Diligence involves reviewing the business plan, interviewing the management, conducting customer reference calls and meetings, conducting technical evaluations and financial modeling. The different components in the diligence process help to create understanding of the business, identify risk factors, and develop strategies to mitigate those risk factors. The strategies for risk mitigation are unique to the business plan. Every company is different, so one looks for ways to minimize capital requirements, accelerate business development in the marketplace, minimize technical and competitive risks, and minimize liabilities. There are a host of risks that one has to identify and come to grips with. Some of those are more applicable than others, depending on the particular business plan and circumstances being evaluated. The risk management plan has to be tailored to the particular circumstances of the opportunity.

After due diligence and risk evaluation, negotiations are the next step. Negotiations involve determining the investment arrangement in a company, which includes negotiating valuation, terms and conditions, board structure, governance matters, and many other provisions associated with the investment. These parameters define the economic structure, the governance structure, the reporting structure, and ongoing management structure of the company. One set of negotiations occurs with the company. If there are co-investors, there is another set of negotiations with the other business partners.

Post-investment management is accomplished through ongoing interface with the company, typically at the board level. It's a combination of both formal and informal reporting interfaces with the company. We give assistance in areas where it's deemed appropriate or useful. These frequently involve overseeing the compensation structures, the audit function of the company, the personnel plans of the company, the reporting structures of the company, strategic partner interfaces, and additional business opportunities. There are a host of activities that go on for months, and sometimes years, that are all intended to accelerate the growth of the company, achieve profitability sooner, and establish a quality organization that is of value.

Concurrent with post-investment management, one also does exit planning. This involves positioning the company both internally and externally for either a trade sale or a public offering. In most cases, it ends up being a trade sale. The exit planning and exit monitoring process drives the ultimate returns.

Raising the Money

None of this deal making would be possible without money. The whole other side of the venture capital business is the capital formation effort, which means raising venture funds that can be invested. It's an ongoing marketing activity of identifying institutional investors, interfacing with the marketplace, staying current with institutional investors, and positioning the venture practice to be able to access capital in the future. At discrete moments, we'll go to market to raise a new fund wherein we specifically market the fund, negotiate the partnership structure, and close on a facility. Once that is accomplished, we create an ongoing set of interfaces to work with our limited partners in those funds. Through those interfaces we keep them informed about what we do, what investments we're making, and how we're tracking those investments.

There are a lot of investor relations activities involved such as simply keeping investors abreast of developments, answering questions, and making courtesy calls. Some limited partnerships are more active than others. Much of the investor relations side is handling the qualitative requirements of a limited partner.

Rules of Venture Capital

Raising money and doing deals are complicated processes with many pitfalls along the way. There are a few general rules that can be used to help ensure success. At its simplest level, it's people, market, competitiveness, and governance. In terms of people, experienced management is critical. That means a complete management team with a capable board of directors that is constructed with an eye toward the needs of the company going forward, rather than legacy kinds of relationships. The board and the management team are critical in establishing functional and creative capabilities for a successful undertaking.

Ensuring that these attributes can or do exist is a key part of the ongoing post-investment management effort. One is never assured that a company will evolve successfully, but diligent assessment and management of an investment seeks to establish a reasonable probability of a successful outcome.

Another key rule is making sure you have an actual marketplace that can be served. Specifically, that means serving a critical need in that marketplace as opposed to a "nice to have." You can have the greatest technology in the world, but if nobody actually needs it, you aren't going to go anywhere. A key parameter that we track is whether there are real customers, and whether the product or service addresses a critical need in the marketplace.

In addition to the marketplace, we also investigate whether the product or service that the company is supplying is in fact providing real value. Is there a clear value proposition? Presuming that there is a need, is the company's solution providing a compelling solution? Does the value proposition stack up competitively in the marketplace? Does the company own its own IP (intellectual property) in order to continually control and refresh that value proposition to maintain a competitive advantage? Are there key people in the company that have the know-how to continually refresh that IP? Does the company really understand corporate controls and corporate governance?

It's also quite important to stay up-to-date on industry trends. To that end, we use a myriad of tools: conferences, studies, networking, reading, visiting with customers, tracking trends, and interfacing with technical advisors, legal advisors, and regulatory advisors. It is an integral part of our strategy, and we have a substantial ongoing research function in our organization as a core capability.

Finally, there is the matter of integrity and trust. Ultimately, you're investing in teams of people to execute an uncertain plan, so you've got to have confidence in the commitment, integrity, and honesty of the people in which you're investing.

Making the Investment

To spot opportunities for investment, our philosophy is that you've got to be a student of the industry sector applicable to the investment. We pick certain industries that we think are the most promising, whether it's telecom, IT, electronics, or others, in which we have experience. The principals of the firm have years, if not decades, of both operational and investment experience associated with these and other industries. With regard to the industries that we choose to serve, the way we've found opportunities is to have talent in our organization that has a deep amount of experience in those industries. We believe we have a unique understanding of our target industries and their trends, both micro and macro. With that approach, we have a better opportunity to spot opportunities or create them.

Exit strategies are an important part of making an investment. The typical liquidation scenario is a trade sale, because it's a more likely outcome. Most venture-backed deals exit through trade sale. Realizing that that's the case, we plan in the large majority of our cases to exit through a trade sale. It's the option that you can most depend on and it's the one for which you can best position. If accomplished correctly, it's also the one that can generate excellent returns in ways that mitigate the downstream capital risk. That doesn't mean that you wouldn't take advantage of an IPO when it makes sense and try to position for it, but you can't plan for it. It's also the case in a public market offering that you're opening yourself up to a lot of market risks that could then dictate what your returns are going to be. In the case of a trade sale, however, you've got a more predictable return model.

Working with Entrepreneurs

Entrepreneurs who are experienced with institutional venture capital are typically more sophisticated in their view of the undertaking. Some of the less experienced entrepreneurs, such as the technology-based founder or the enthusiastic young adult, aren't typically aware or sensitive to all the things that have to happen correctly for a business to be successful. Entrepreneurs that are institutionally experienced are going to pre-think issues about what valuation should really be, what kind of option pool structure you really need, what kind of timeline is realistic in milestones of the company, what kind of capital requirements are realistic, and many other factors that can determine success. With lesser-experienced entrepreneurs, you typically end up with differences of opinion on valuation, control issues, governance, and other issues.

Common Mistakes

It's crucial to learn from one's own mistakes, as well as from common mistakes that are made. A lot of entrepreneurs typically overvalue their investment, and under-appreciate the challenge of building or growing their business.

Another common mistake is inadequate or incomplete risk assessment, which typically results in failure. Surprises for which you're not prepared can kill a company. Another big mistake is misjudgment of management capabilities. This issue is fairly high on the list of common VC mistakes.

Undercapitalizing the venture is another common mistake as well as optimistic timing. Over-forecasting and under-resourcing are typically common mistakes entrepreneurs make.

The Management Team

To avoid the aforementioned mistakes, experience is the most important thing we look for in a management team. It's a team approach. You're not necessarily going to find all the skills you are looking for in one single person, so we approach it from the standpoint of building functional teams. This applies whether it is a board of directors or a management team. The skills you're looking for are knowledge and recognized leadership in the technology domain that is involved, knowledge of the market and the customers that are going to be served, and knowledge of how to build and develop an organization.

At the board level, we look for a combination of board members that can contribute to the strategic direction of the company and create access in the marketplace to assist the company in accelerating its business development or networking needs. We like board members that have direct, applicable experience in the kind of business in which we're investing.

The venture capitalist typically works with the CEO and other key members of the management team to track the performance of the company against the business plan on a monthly, quarterly, and annual basis. It is important to build a working relationship with the CEO to achieve clear communication and early warning input of issues. This assists the venture capitalist to help advise and guide a CEO through some of the more major decisions of the company. This working relationship is achieved through both a formal reporting structure and an informal relationship to serve as a trusted advisor of the company.

To some extent, the same parameters apply to working with the other senior managers, in a somewhat lesser way. One has to have a relationship with the CTO, CFO, CIO, COO, or other key members of the management team, but those relationships have to be tempered by keeping an environment where the CEO can maintain leadership over the organization. Clearly one has to build a comfort level with the other key members of the management team to maintain dialogue, balanced by the assurance that you're not micromanaging the situation.

When working with board members, clearly there has to be trust in their judgment. The majority of the key decisions occur during board meetings and meetings of committees of the board. You're looking to other board members to provide insightful solutions. To have a properly functioning board, it has to have members that work well in a team environment, that are forthcoming in a consensus-building environment, and that can provide real advice, counsel, insight, and direction on matters particularly associated with their experience.

Factors Affecting Investment Decisions

There are many factors that affect the decision to invest. One of the most critical factors is the stage of development of the company looking for funds. Depending on what stage the company is, the process is going to be different. A seed stage company would be approached differently than a late stage situation. The stage of the company will change the kind of risk factors, diligence activities, or post-investment objectives on which one focuses. We are generally not a seed stage investor as these ventures are typically too early for us. We like to see situations that are a little bit more mature. Ideally there will already be some customers and the primary use of proceeds will be expansion as opposed to entering the market.

We occasionally do what's called an early stage deal, which is generally pre-revenue or still in negative cash flow. Along with the stage of the company, we also look at the size. Generally, stage and size go hand in hand. As the stages progress, the size increases—if it's working. If it's not increasing, you've got a different situation.

Another factor to consider in an investment decision is profitability. A profitable company has more options than a company that is not profitable, or in positive cash flow. As venture capitalists, most of the companies in which we invest are not yet profitable and are likely still in negative cash flow. In the majority of the situations at which we look, a company is in a high growth situation that requires capital to support that growth rate. Once a company is cash flow positive, other alternatives for financing growth open up, such as debt financing, bank financing, mezzanine financing, and potentially even public market financing.

When the Economy Goes Sour

The state of the economy will affect a company looking for funds. The exact effect of a down economy depends on the company and their market. You can make money in up markets and down markets; it depends on what kind of service you're providing. For the kind of markets we serve, a general economy that's in a downward trend is not positive. You're generally going to grow faster in an economy that's stable or growing. You can occasionally get a counter-cyclical circumstance where a down economy is actually increasing the need for improved productivity. In that situation, an entrepreneur could actually enjoy growth and prosper in a down market. It depends on the particular circumstances of the venture.

We try to mitigate risk associated with the general economy by focusing on companies that provide a viable value proposition that is meeting a true need. In such situations, volatility associated with overall market conditions is somewhat mitigated. The assumption is that if the company or product is meeting a true need, that need is not going to go away based on the volatility of the general market conditions. Of course, that statement only holds true if we've chosen our markets and companies well.

Growth Potential

In a company in which we're investing, we look for high growth potential. Ideally, we're looking for 50 percent or more a year. Now, that's an unusual company, and the reality is that we've done deals with a projected growth in the 20 to 30 percent a year range. We're not going to invest in a company that, if all else is equal, is going to grow at 5 percent a year. We're looking for a company that can achieve extraordinary growth in a relatively short period of time.

We evaluate the potential return in the context of the projected operating profile against the capital required to achieve that plan. We match that up against what we perceive a value might be from accomplishing that plan through various means. We'll do classic modeling on return potential, with a lot of sensitivity testing the volatility in terms of value.

Risk assessment involves more than the capital risk. There are organizational development risks, technology risks, market risks, competitive risks, and regulatory risks that have to be considered. There are a host of risks that we try to model consistent with the financial model to get a sense of what our risk profile is. We try to determine how that's going to change over time, and what the company needs to be doing to prepare for, manage, and hopefully mitigate those risks.

We do a lot of contingency planning, and a lot of reserve planning. We tend to look at things conservatively, and ensure that we have a resilient risk management plan. For example, our reserve policy is fairly substantial. When we go into a company, we're reserving additional capital equal to or often greater than the amount that we initially invest just to mitigate the capital risk.

Determining Valuations

When determining a valuation, we start at zero. We want to own 100 percent and put no money in. The upper valuation boundary is infinity; that is, the entrepreneur wants to own 100 percent and you give him all the money you have. This means valuation is ultimately a negotiated solution. We'll look at any number of methodologies to guide the discussion: comparables, stage of development of the company, amount that's been invested, value of the assets, discounted cash flow models, pro forma projections, and many others. We look at all those things and ultimately come to an informed judgment as to what a rational valuation is for the company. Our judgment is then tempered by negotiations with the company. Ultimately it can be a competitive issue. There could be other investors that perceive the company as more valuable than we do and start bidding up the price. In that situation, we need to make a decision as to how competitive we want to be. All the traditional financial tools are tempered by negotiations and the competitive environment to create a market-based valuation.

In different situations, companies will have different factors affecting the valuation decision. For example, in the case of a start-up company with only an idea but a solid management team, a primary determinant might be what we think the capital structure needs to look like to support the initial growth of the company. We will also understand the partnership nature of the investment to keep the incentive in the structure for the founders and management, with an ample amount of ownership reserve to support the growth of the company. We work hard to try to achieve fair structures that properly compensate us for the risk capital, and at the same time create an environment where everyone is mutually incented for a successful outcome. That mean the valuation needs to be high enough to motivate the founders, but low enough to allow some growth potential in valuation as the company starts to perform. It's rare that you can find a deal where only one round of capital is sufficient. As a result, you've got to think about the first round in the context of the overall capital needs of the company over some reasonable period of time, then scale the first round to be consistent with the capital plan to support the company. Generally speaking, it's a relatively low amount of capital for a relatively high percentage of the company that then gets diluted over time.

In the case of a company with significant sales, profits, and prior rounds of funding and plans to go public, we'd look carefully at publicly traded comparables, large private equity rounds, and mezzanine transactions on comparable or even larger size transactions. As part of the evaluation, we'd have a lot of conversations with the investment banking community on what they perceive the relative merits of the situation to be vis-à-vis other traded comparables. In that case, you'd put a lot of weight on a comparative analysis.

John Higginbotham is the founder and chairman of SpaceVest. He was formerly a co-founder, director, and senior vice president of International Technology Underwriters, Inc. (INTEC), a premier space and telecommunications insurance underwriting management company, now owned and operated by the AXA Insurance Company as AXASpace. Earlier in his career, Mr. Higginbotham was the product manager for Hewlett Packard Company's global entry into the microcomputer industry. Mr. Higginbotham received his B.S. degree in civil engineering with honors from Virginia Tech and his M.B.A. from Harvard Business School. Mr. Higginbotham serves as the chairman of the Space Foundation, a global non-profit organization supporting space activities, space professionals, and education.

Creating Success in the Venture Capital Industry

Jon Staenberg

Partner
Rustic Canyon

Introduction

While there are billions of dollars at stake, venture capital really isn't about the money—it's about the business and the relationships. Venture capitalists are in the business of providing expert counsel and services to both portfolio companies and investors. The great thing about this business is that the audiences we want to support and help succeed—investors and portfolio companies—are not at odds with each other. In fact, we're all pulling for the same thing: creating a platform that ensures success. Investors want to see the portfolio companies succeed just as much as the companies want to succeed. A good venture fund actually picks its investors, making sure that a number of them also provide more than just money. Often investors can help the companies directly, too. It's a win-win situation. In the end, is money a motivator? To some degree, yes. But if that's your only motivator, you won't be in the business long.

A day in the life of....

Rustic Canyon Partners is a firm like no other. Rustic Canyon Partners invests in companies positioned for strong growth. We look for companies that capitalize on opportunities created by technology change, market evolution, regulatory shifts, or other factors. We have invested in a broad array of technology-driven and middle-market companies in sectors such as communications, software, IT infrastructure, business and information services, materials science, and efficient energy.

As a venture capital firm, our most obvious investment is capital but our most differentiating investment is time. With a high ratio of partners to capital under management, the firm makes a significant investment of partner time and expertise in the disciplined sourcing, evaluation, and due diligence work we do prior to making a decision to invest. Additionally, our team brings experience from a broad range of areas including direct start-up experience, seed investments, legal expertise, and mergers and acquisitions. So, once an investment is made, we have the expertise and drive to support our companies and help them flourish.

The foundation of Rustic Canyon's investment and management process is the following:

- Two partners with complementary skills follow each investment opportunity.
- All partners review and approve each investment opportunity.
- We participate in building our portfolio companies; we are closely aligned with management and active in the boardroom.
- We leverage our broad and deep network to accelerate the growth of our portfolio companies.

As hands-on investors seeking to add significant value to our portfolio companies, we generally require board representation and have a preference for companies based near our footprint of operations in the west coast. Our partners include professionals with varied, complementary backgrounds and our due diligence process includes the practice of having two partners work with each of our new investments. We work collaboratively, making all the decisions as a team and are dedicated to two guiding principles: building successful companies and providing superior returns to the investors who have entrusted us with their capital.

My typical day is split in three ways:

- Working on existing investments
- Hearing about new potential investments
- Creating and fostering relationships to help the first two

What I love about this is that all of these are interrelated and often doing one will help the other. If I am hearing about a new company, it may spur me to think about how one of our existing companies is doing business. Helping an existing portfolio company may show me an area of customer pain that is not being addressed by the market.

I have little separation between my business and personal life. I always think there is more I can do to help my companies and am so passionate about this work that I am more than happy to make my social life include my venture world.

Venture capital seeks to make a significant, and at times revolutionary, impact to economies and quality of life. Venture capital professionals are in the business to support the entrepreneurs on the front lines. Perhaps we won't become famous, but we'll hopefully be the foundation for new ideas and long-lasting companies. In the end, we want to make a difference for our investors, our companies, and the world at large.

The Team

As is the case in almost all business settings, politics, and sports, the people that surround you are crucial for success. The team is the driving force behind companies that perform and companies that don't. Colleagues at a venture capital firm are key sources of information and advice that guide investment decisions. Entrepreneurs and venture capitalists need to bring a team to the table with the talent and experience to manage the day-to-day tasks of running a company and, at the same time, see the long-term challenges of building a company.

Team members need to be able to identify the most promising opportunities, advise a start up's management team, and always seek ways to gain new knowledge, expand a network of allies, and create a platform where deal flow is robust.

I remember one of the first deals I ever did. I met a twenty-six-year-old entrepreneur, and after thirty minutes, I said I would invest. If I can find the right leader, who is full of integrity, passion, vision, and a maniacal fear of failure, I will be on that person. He didn't disappoint.

Doing the Deal

When thinking about deals, there are two main focuses. One is to help create proprietary deal flow and ensure that we're reviewing all the good opportunities. The second is the actual work that goes into identifying and researching the opportunities in order to make good decisions. You have to do your homework in this business. That's one of the things people got away from in the dot-com era—firms were competing over every deal and rushing to do deals. To succeed today, a lot of work goes into trying to identify the truly exceptional ones. Warren Buffett, one of my heroes, points out that unlike baseball, you don't have to swing until you get that one pitch you love. Not doing certain deals can be as important as choosing to do others.

Getting out of the office and meeting with entrepreneurs is also one of the keys to success in this business. Not only are you actually hearing from the innovators, but you're also building recognition in the industry as "entrepreneur friendly." We really celebrate the entrepreneur and we want to help the entrepreneur. Even if a company is not ready for our investment, I will meet with them if the entrepreneur has vision. I'm continually meeting with people I know that we're not going to invest in at the time. Maybe later down the road this person will be ready for our investment, with the same company or another one. Spending time with them, asking the right questions about their idea, and exploring how to take it to the next level of getting funding is important. There are some basic aspects of setting up a company. You want to accelerate the path to revenue and these are the kinds of things to do to help that.

Some of the best deal flow is created by being close to folks with really great ideas and a passion for startups. We speak on panels and do proprietary research in a variety of different sectors to try to identify additional opportunities. Every day I'm learning. Information is available about deals and industry trends and possible growth opportunities so it becomes critically important to be proactive in your quest for more information. Where are you going to find the next deal? How can you become more of an expert? How can you increase this incredibly powerful network to bring in more ideas and more opportunities?

The Team, the Market, and the Technology

Once the potential investment is identified, a lot of due diligence is required. People always talk about two things in the big picture of investing: the team and the market. Both these aspects will give you plenty of work in a day.

Before investing in a company, it is important to spend significant time with the team. The team ultimately has to drive the ship. Good chemistry is imperative. Team members have to respect each other, have experience, and demonstrate clear passion and the ability to react. In the start-up world, you walk through the door any given day and you don't exactly know what that day is going to hold. If a team is flexible and able to react quickly while still maintaining the big picture, then you have the elements for a successful team.

Understanding the market is critical. The management team is something to examine, but even the best team simply can't succeed if the market just isn't right. There is some flexibility in how one can adjust a team to better excel but the fact is, if the market isn't there, it probably won't work. If a market is not big, it is hard to make it big. Therefore, you spend a lot of time understanding what the addressable market is and the trends of the markets.

The other thing to consider is who are the obvious buyers? Sometimes competition is a really good thing because it creates potential buyers of a new technology or company. All of those things go into the equation. We are hoping to find companies that can grow to be a certain size. This is a little bit like baseball where the all-star hitter is the guy hitting .300. If you can get three out of ten deals that have the kind of outcome that you want, the investors will be happy.

Being reactive and being proactive are important when trying to spot an opportunity. You need to be ready when the opportunity comes and to actually know the players and the trends in various industries. Having access and utilizing a broad range of experts and analysts and research services is key to preparing yourself. When the right opportunity comes to the door, you want to be ready for it.

It is important to be proactive: take a look at the world, identify unmet needs and/or problems, and work to address them. At the end of the day, the people we want to hear from most are entrepreneurs who are close to the market or in the market. They are attractive because their ideas are not based on research and analysis; they are based on being out in the world.

Another aspect of due diligence is simply knowing the product. Our firm does early stage IT investing. Technology is critical in that equation, so we need to know the technology. Our team relies on a range of advisors and experts. An individual team can't know everything, but if you know where to look and who to tap for specific issues, that network can exponentially broaden your knowledge base. We use people who have been CTOs or CIOs, and who really can understand whether the technology works and whether this team can create great technology, and the unique assets of this technology. Our advisory board is a group of colleagues with whom we have close working relationships or prior transactional experience. We rely on their expertise. These individuals alert us to emerging IT trends affecting the businesses of tomorrow, advise us on new technologies, and consult with us during the due diligence phase of our investment process.

With so many venture funds out there investing in IT, you need to ask yourself what is it that your portfolio companies are creating that is different from other entrepreneurs? More importantly, is your investment helping solve a true problem?

We spend a lot of time sizing up a market and looking at the role of technology by talking to customers and potential customers. At Rustic Canyon, it is really the confluence of the team, the market and the product—in this case, technology—and how it relates to that market.

Three Keys to an Exceptional Investment

Understanding the team, the market, and the technology gives you a good insight into an investment opportunity. But we're not looking for just any good investment; our firm is out there looking for exceptional investments. We're working as hard as we can, trying to identify the investment that will provide a big return. To find those exceptional investments, three factors come into play: the science, the art, and the unfair advantage.

Our team approaches opportunities with both a scientific approach and an artistic approach. Value to metrics, analyzing numbers and data, and market indicators are the scientific part. We are extremely valuation sensitive. There are many venture funds chasing a lot of deals—you have to be analytical in this business. Taking an industry analysis and comparing valuations or other deals that have been done around a certain space is one way to understand an opportunity. We look at both private and public market valuation and contrast that to our opportunity. That is the science part of it.

There is also an art. You have to decide what is fair and what is appropriate when dealing with a company. What is appropriate given the team's experience and the size of the idea? Are you giving the team enough valuation to motivate them? When do you need to press and when do you need to back off and give them room? The art is utilizing psychology and sociology; it's nothing more than people skills. Also, the art of this work involves seeing the bigger picture and having a strategic vision. It's appropriate to know the end game. What can you say at the end of the day if things go according to plan or close to it? What kind of return on investment are we looking at? Be realistic but always have goals for specific companies.

Finally, creating successful opportunities means creating an unfair advantage. An unfair advantage is something that differentiates a company from every other one; it is something they can do uniquely that others can't do. All successful companies need something that makes it hard to sell against them, and makes it easier for them to differentiate themselves from competitors. What are the resources, the assets, or the skills that the company can bring to any deal?

And the unfair advantage principle applies for our business, too. It applies to Rustic Canyon just as much as it applies to a portfolio company. What's our unfair advantage as a venture capital firm? Given the fact that we have extensive deal experience in venture capital and a unique geographical positioning covering the entire west coast, we're able to strategically leverage those traits and the access to those markets, and create for ourselves that same unfair advantage we look for in start-up companies. It helps us sell ourselves to the companies we hope to invest in, too.

We're also unique in that we're collaborators. Unlike some venture firms, we are interested in what other venture funds are doing and how we can work together. We think that having more smart and experienced people around the table is better. We're always interested in talking to both investors and seasoned executives and technologists who have domain expertise in the areas we're looking at. Other people who can bring a dimension of experience or skill around the table are only going to help the deal.

Putting Resources to Work

At Rustic Canyon, our partners have enough broad experience in this business that there's always something that we can help entrepreneurs with every day. Common issues range from operational, funding, sales and marketing, or technology challenges. Every day, every one of these areas presents itself as the classic fork in the road moment for a portfolio company. As partners with a lot of experience, we can get into the issue and say, "I've been here before, I've overcome this obstacle, here's my advice." We're able to focus just on that question and help the entrepreneur and the team find the answer that we know is there.

No two days are ever alike. Day to day, my tasks range from working on a specific company issue to meeting with a broad set of people to better understand a company's strengths and discuss its vision. It's everything from the granular to the big picture. Some firms believe it's just about showing up once a month to a board meeting, doing a checklist, and walking away. At Rustic Canyon, we're looking to add value to the company. And we're looking to add value in every way. We want them to succeed as much as they want to succeed.

Rules of the Game

There are no mysteries to creating success in the venture capital business. It is a lot of hard work and problem solving. And it's also about selling and leading. Everyone has to walk away feeling that they are entering into the best possible partnership. Successful partnerships are about being human, working hard, and keeping your integrity. People sometimes forget these key human characteristics because the start-up world moves at such a fast pace. Everyone knows there are certain venture funds that have the cache of being above the rest. It is not about that. It is really about the team. It is about the group showing up every day and being engaged and adding value for the company.

One of the rules of the game is that the entrepreneur should interview the VC as much as the VC is doing their due diligence on the entrepreneur and the investment opportunity. Some VCs will overfund the company. You want to do what is right for the company and so often that is lost. There are many agendas at play during an investment opportunity. Growing a long-lasting company is the goal and you won't get there if you lose focus on what really matters in this business. Building and sustaining relationships with the entrepreneur, the team, and your investors is critical.

Relationship with the Key Players

One particularly interesting relationship is that with the CEO. Working with the CEO in a venture-backed company is a relationship of mutual respect and collaboration. You have to be able to direct and guide, as appropriate, as different situations and challenges come up. But first, you need to make sure the right CEO is in place.

The single most important function of the board is to make sure that the right CEO is guiding the ship. This is the nature of business, and some are better positioned to lead at certain points of a company's growth than others. Look at Bill Gates as one of the great examples. He stepped down as CEO to go back to his true passion—development—acknowledging that Steve Ballmer was better equipped to guide Microsoft as the maturing blue chip it had become. More often, however, it is the board that needs to recognize when it is time for a CEO change to occur and how to execute that change properly. The board should see the future and vision of the company and find the CEO best situated for that direction accordingly. At times this might require removing the founder who has led the company and finding that person a more suitable role—a very fragile scenario. If done well, it can be a smooth transition. If executed poorly you could have not only a disgruntled founder who won't contribute, but also a tenuous and inefficient beginning for the new CEO. This is the psychology of entrepreneurship and part of our job is to handle this with respect and expediency.

Once the CEO is in place, you must trust, support, and help implement their vision and style of leadership. Giving a CEO the room to do what he or she does well is important. The CEO is a lonely position. Being able to provide a sounding board, a place where CEOs can discuss their concerns, is a role that needs to be played by the board and investment team as well.

It is truly a team effort that makes this work. The team must function well together. You need to make sure that members of the board have a touch point into various members of the senior management team. In some ways, these are tough, lonely positions at the top of an organizational chart and you need a place to check in. That is critical for the success of a startup.

Common Mistakes

One mistake that entrepreneurs often make is they lack the inability to step back in a fast-paced start-up situation to assess where the company needs to go. This is why having a good VC as a trusted mentor really helps.

I always encourage the company to do due diligence on the VC as the VC does due diligence on them. Ask hard questions like, what will you do to add value, when are you available, what past examples can you point to, what is your vision for yourselves and for us, etc. And hold them to their answers! Again, if you are just taking money, you are being shortchanged.

In terms of hiring, there is undue pressure to get the next hire done versus making the right hire. The wrong hire in an early stage company is costly because if you are a four-person company and one of the people is not working out, that is 25 percent of your company. Venture capital advisors need to help entrepreneurs get it right.

A common mistake that venture capitalists make is that they rely too much on their past performance. Sometimes VCs look at this more as a funding task rather than what it really is—a business development task. That is a no-win scenario.

Minimizing Risk

Living the life of a venture capitalist is not for the faint of heart. What we try to do is take a risky investment proposition, with many unknowns, and create some certainty, some element of reduced risk. We do that by really being close to a market, understanding that market, and working with people you have worked in it before with.

Buffett talks about the "unfair advantage," and Andy Grove says that only "the paranoid survive." If in the beginning we haven't created some unique differentiator for us, then the race is over before we started and we will not win. If we aren't constantly vigilant going forward, we will be blindsided.

Conclusion

In our office, we have created an art gallery dedicated to the great entrepreneurs and the companies they have created. We wrote an intro to it that summarizes how we feel:

The beginnings are all the same. They begin with only an idea and the belief that that idea can withstand the rapids of commerce. It is the bold who move from the idea to action, relying on their wits, family and friends. Powered by determination, elbow grease, capital and sometimes even luck, young start-up businesses test their strength in new territories. As the icon of the H-P garage reminds us, some ideas are so powerful they have to be expressed, no matter how humble their beginnings might be. This is the entrepreneurial landscape that has made American business and created now-familiar brands that, in their beginnings were once just an idea conjured over lunch on the face of a napkin or an inspiration in a conversation between friends. This show, mostly focused on the companies in our region, celebrates those humble beginnings and the people who have spun their ideas into gold. Ultimately, the show celebrates our passion for entrepreneurs, their ideas and the belief that we can change the world by helping build the next generation of great companies. We are reserving plenty of wall space and frames for their future successes.

This business probably seems so sexy to outsiders. And during the bubble, lots of folks got in. Many of those same people are now out, looking for other things to do. I have done this for a decade and plan to do it for another decade. People often ask me how it is going and I always say, ask me in a few years. But day to day, it is the people and technology and the unwavering belief that this stuff makes a difference that keeps me smiling.

Jon Staenberg, a partner at Rustic Canyon, has been working with venture-backed companies for more than a decade. In this capacity, he has started his own company, worked full time in other companies, and consulted to over fifty startups. He is one of the most experienced venture capitalists in the Pacific Northwest, having raised two funds *totaling over $100 million. After working in the marketing area at Microsoft for six years, he joined Virtual i-O as VP of Sales & Marketing. During the last eight years, he has been engaged in business planning, business development, financial planning and fundraising, recruiting and M&A work for a variety of Silicon Valley and Seattle-based startups. Mr. Staenberg serves on the boards of Class.com and Micropath, and is on the advisory boards of New Vine Logistics, Vista Broadband, Prime Advantage, Time Domain, Atlantes.com, OneName, Syncronex, and uReach.com. He graduated Phi Beta Kappa from Stanford University, where he received his B.S., M.A., and M.B.A.*

The Many Layers of Venture Capital

Graham Burnette

General Partner

SBV Venture Partners

SBV Venture Partners is a relatively small venture fund—less than $50 million—so each general partner must perform many functions. Over the life of the fund, my distinct functions fall into five major categories: (1) raising the fund's money, (2) sourcing deals, (3) using the due diligence process to reduce the large number of potential investments into those that actually become the companies in the portfolio, (4) working with portfolio companies as they grow to help them become profitable, successful ventures, and (5) creating a liquidity event and determining the timing of that event.

1. Strategies for Raising Money

In terms of fundraising, SBV is a bit out of the mainstream in that we did not raise money from the typical U.S. institutional investors and endowment funds. SBV is the third in a family of funds, following Euro-America I and Euro-America II. Many of SBV's limited partners are European institutions that are interested in Silicon Valley. Partly, this is to give them visibility of what is happening in Silicon Valley and partly to get an early leg up on creating relationships with those companies that they hope will grow and become major partners in the future.

In addition to our fundraising in Europe, a pension fund from Canada and a financial institution from Japan are also major investors. We are very pleased that we have relationships with investors from throughout the world involved in SBV. This gives the fund a perspective that we would not otherwise have.

In our experience, the most important single item in our fundraising process was determining why each potential investor was investing in venture capital. Before the bubble days, most of us never thought about this. After the bubble burst, we discovered that people and institutions invest in venture capital for many disparate reasons. The people who invest just because they think it is a wonderful way to make gobs of money in a short period became upset as soon as we got into a down cycle. Those investors are no longer investing in venture.

A venture capitalist needs to make sure that the limited partners and general partners have alignment of interest over the course of the fund's existence.

In essence, the general partners and the investors need to make sure they have a common view of general strategy to be followed over the course of that fund's lifetime.

2. Sourcing Deals

Most deals get sourced through the personal networks of venture capitalists. We are certainly no different in terms of our deal sourcing. At SBV, we have two general partners, Jacques Vallee and myself. Jacques has a very broad personal network that goes back to when he was one of the principle investigators for Arpanet while working at SRI and through being an active venture capital investor for over twenty years.

I have a different background. I am trained as a lawyer and worked in Silicon Valley with connections in the legal, accounting, and investment banking industries. I then stopped practicing law to become CFO of one of my former clients, a company named Mercury Interactive, where I was the CFO leading up to and through the IPO. Now Mercury is a very successful company and a member of the S&P 500.

Jacques and I bring two broad personal networks with little overlap because our backgrounds are different. People in our personal networks bring potential deals to SBV because they see something in a company raising money that makes them think about Jacques or me. We track how many of these deals come to us through our personal networks and through other means. We typically look at about 1,300 to 1,400 deals each year. Over four years of making investments, SBV has made only seventeen investments. Less than one-half of one percent of the deals we examine result in an investment.

3. Due Diligence

Jacques and I are only two men and no matter how smart or experienced we are, we don't know enough to do the due diligence on all of these companies ourselves. We are experts in certain areas and, in those areas, we know whether something has been done or if it has problems. In other areas, however, we have to go to our network of advisors for help in due diligence. SBV has a formal board of advisors comprised of experts in several areas. We have aggressively sought at least one person, but usually two or three, who is an expert in most of the substantive areas in which we are likely to look at companies. If a business opportunity seems to make sense to us, we ask the appropriate advisor if that business is built on real science. Similarly, we also have advisors who are marketing experts.

Before we go too far into due diligence on any company, it has to meet three criteria. First, it must have a management team in which we feel confident. Even the best business plan can't be followed like a recipe. Business plans show how well a management team thinks and analyzes but they don't provide a roadmap for building a company. We have to depend on the management team to know when to vary from the business plan, tear it up, and make a new plan. That requires a substantial amount of business expertise and knowledge.

Second, the market has to be major and the company, if successful, has to provide real value. Typically, this means that the company has to solve some sort of significant problem that people really care about. If people don't care enough about a problem to pay hard dollars for the solution, even a company that is dramatically successful in creating their product will fail in business.

Third, the company needs a way to defend itself once it becomes successful. Companies must have a plan for becoming successful and preventing others from copying the idea and taking the business. Since most of our companies are based on some aspect of technology, they usually defend themselves by protecting their intellectual property. We don't slavishly require each company to have a portfolio of patents because we are more concerned with the goal, rather than IP for its own sake.

We conduct a structured analysis as we look at each of these elements. The analysis serves as the first hurdle before real due diligence.

Our next step involves financial modeling of a potential company. We look at the entrepreneur's predictions, but we tend to find that our own models are more accurate. Entrepreneurs have to be incredibly optimistic. The chances of a company succeeding are so small that if the founder wasn't a wild-eyed optimist, he or she would never give up a good paying job to go and start a new company. We encourage that optimism, so we never argue directly with an entrepreneur about his or her projections for the company. We do, however, make our own projections, modeling whether, when, and how large a liquidity event might ultimately result from an investment.

In a very small percentage of the companies, the due diligence process convinces us to make an investment.

4. Helping the Company Grow

SBV does not invest in a company unless we believe that we can help the company grow and focus its energy on what will make it succeed. If we only brought dollars, we would have nothing unique to offer and we wouldn't get a premium for the risk involved. We can lessen the risk, however, by bringing in our own expertise. We think that our fund has good returns because we are able to buy into a company when the risks are high, use our expertise to help that company overcome risks, and benefit from high returns.

When it comes to helping a company grow, Jacques and I draw heavily from our own personal experiences. In addition to the work that he did with Stanford and Stanford Research Institute, Jacques has founded his own technology-based start-up company and has worked with startups as a venture capital investor for over twenty years. He has seen many companies succeed and even more fail, and the failures teach more than the successes. I have seen similar successes and failures through my work as a lawyer for start-up technology companies, as a CFO of a company that went public, and then founding my own company that successfully sold its technology. Between the two of us, we have a broad experiential base of good and bad decisions that we can bring to companies in the SBV portfolio.

5. Liquidity

Over the last five years, liquidity has been the most difficult step in the life of a start-up company. The public stock market drives most liquidity events, either directly or indirectly, because if the company does not have a public offering potential, it is unlikely that it will have an acquisition liquidity event at an attractive value.

During the past four years, public markets have not been receptive to liquidity events in the form of IPOs. This has caused SBV to work differently with companies. In the current environment, companies must grow at a slower rate than they did during the late 1990s. We help companies avoid developing an appetite for cash that we can't fill. We have slowed down the growth of several of our companies in hopes of matching the company development with the receptiveness of the public markets. This has worked out nicely. Two of our companies whose growth was slowed suddenly became attractive takeover candidates to large publicly traded companies who swooped in and made preemptive acquisition offers that have turned into our liquidity events.

VC – A Relationship Business

The business of venture capital is a business of relationships with other people. Investors in the fund, entrepreneurs, other executives at portfolio companies, co-investors in companies, advisors—the list of relationships that can make or break the fund is almost endless.

Common Situations with Entrepreneurs

Every company is unique. Every entrepreneur I ever worked with has always been incredibly bright and has been successful his or her entire life. Not surprisingly, entrepreneurs tend to be confident in themselves and their abilities. This confidence tends to make entrepreneurs think they can do more than they really can. The transition for first-time entrepreneurs from being a superstar inside a large organization to being on their own and struggling can be difficult. Thus, they often need a strong relationship with a mentor that can help them make the transition.

Entrepreneurs can take for granted the ability to make things happen in a large organization. Limited resources and tight staffing change the world as they shift to a startup. This is the main reason that venture capitalists talk about focus like a laser: You have to accomplish task number one before you work on number two. Then, you have to make sure that the second item is done before you work on the third item and so on. Stated another way, a start-up entrepreneur must both choose the right tasks and also place them in the right order. Early on, we spend a lot of time working with founding teams to identify the key success variables in their business plan and the required steps to accomplish each of those items. Usually, management uses a triage process—of the ten things we all agree absolutely have to get done, we can only afford to do three. They have to ask, "What are the three that will allow us to survive until tomorrow so that we can still worry about the other seven?"

Forming a Relationship with the CEO

The relationship between investor and CEO differs in every situation. Some CEOs in our portfolio are first timers. Although very accomplished with high expectations for themselves, these entrepreneurs usually recognize the value of mentors and investors who have either run their own companies or have been involved with many companies. While every CEO does not have a mentor/mentee relationship with each investor, he or she usually develops such a relationship with several investors or board members.

Of the thirteen companies in the SBV portfolio, I have close, mentoring relationships with five CEOs. That doesn't mean that I don't like the other CEOs in our portfolio; I just don't have that personal connection. Some look to other investors as mentors. The close relationships become almost like a sibling relationship.

Relationships with Other Executives

We do not limit the personal relationships to the CEOs, but rather proactively seek out the entire founding team. Beyond the founders and the CEOs, we have dramatically fewer relationships. Sometimes relationships exist because I have recruited people from my own personal network for a company. We try to avoid making the CEO feel as if a member of his board is going around him talking to the people on his staff, but we do get deeply involved in the major issues facing companies in our portfolio. For example, it is quite common for us to spend intensive time with VPs of engineering when companies are having problems developing their products or to spend time with VPs of marketing when companies struggle with the right way to introduce a product into a market.

The Multi-Faceted Venture Industry

Many entrepreneurs do not realize that venture capital is not one industry. Venture capital is at least three different sub-industries and probably even more than that. Angel investing is an entire industry itself. We don't participate in angel investing, but we have some strong partnerships with angel organizations. Without angels, some good companies would never get off the ground. Those investors tend to rely on faith in a concept and less on hard due diligence than institutional venture investors do, but they are also people who have successfully built companies of their own. When they have a "gut feeling" that something is a good idea, it usually is.

At the other end, really large venture funds that tend to invest in companies that are already selling, have a defensible technology, and have a major market in an entire industry. This group builds the company to get to a liquidity event. SBV is too small to have an impact in that part of venture capital. Our place is after the angels and before the mezzanine financings. We typically invest in a company when it is still developing the product or just introducing it to the marketplace.

An additional sub-segment of venture capital is what I call "financial engineering." Several very successful venture funds are filled with very smart people with M.B.A.s or engineering backgrounds, but who have not run companies. They figure out how to structure an existing company to make money and are often very good at creating value. At SBV, we are simply not a large enough fund to do financial engineering. If a fund has $500 million or billion dollars, it can develop financial rules that will work on an average basis. But a fund that has about $50 million, like SBV, has to work hard on each company to maximize its chances of success.

That brings us to the world in which SBV operates. In our world, venture capitalists help select from the many competing company concepts and decide which to finance. Even though each individual fund makes those financing decisions independently, the industry as a whole often seems to move in lockstep to support certain types of companies at the same time.

At SBV, once we invest in a company we use our experience and expertise to help portfolio companies turn our investment money into value. We believe that the best venture investors focus less on creating dollar returns, and more on creating value to society in general. When we do our job well, our portfolio companies create something of value, which generates value for our venture fund.

In our portfolio, for example, we had a company called NanoGram, which developed a technology for creating and using nanopowders. Nanopowders are powders in which each grain of a powder is very small, typically just a small number of molecules. Company scientists figured out how to take these fine powders and use laser deposition to move the pieces of powder grain by grain to create batteries in a lattice structure that would hold lots of energy. We discussed the best way to use this technology to build a company. Energy is used in a lot of areas. Some financial models showed you could make the most money by making super capacitors for long distance energy storage. You could also build batteries for laptop computers and cell phones that would last longer and be smaller. Nanogram finally decided to create a spin-off called Nanogram Devices to build better batteries for defibrillators and pacemakers.

A typical pacemaker battery lasts one and a half to two years. Replacing the battery involves open heart surgery. Nanogram Devices developed a battery that would last five years instead of two, cutting the number of open-heart surgeries in half. We thought that offered tremendous value to society. Even before the company got these new implantable batteries to market, the leading company for implantable batteries bought Nanogram Devices based on the first run of prototypes. The company generated a five-times return in a fourteen-month period because it chose the right market. We didn't choose it for dollars and cents reasons. We chose it because that market created the most value for society in general. If you do that right, you create value and the value turns into dollars on its own.

How a Company Should Select its Investors

The stage at which a company raises funds should determine to whom they talk and how they present themselves for financing. A company that only has an idea and still needs to raise money to prove its concept needs to talk to angels. When a company has a proven idea but needs to figure out how to manufacture it inexpensively enough that it can be sold at a price that makes sense, executives need to talk to a different type of an investor. When a company is selling a substantial amount of products and needs to raise money to double or triple the sales force and accelerate their growth, they need to talk to yet a different type of an investor.

SBV does not expect most of the companies presenting to us to be profitable; many of them are not even selling their products yet. A company that is not yet profitable but is trying to invest to accelerate sales growth needs to have a really good explanation of how sales growth will produce profitable operations. Otherwise, why invest?

How company executives present themselves comes into play, as well. At SBV, we have three things that we absolutely require before we will look seriously at a company: a strong management team, a market large enough to generate substantial returns, and a way to defend their business from competitors once they succeed. Most other institutional investors have similar requirements, and are happy to share those requirements with companies.

Company executives should research the requirements of potential investors, compare those requirements with their company, and focus only on those investors that match the company. Then, they should critically self-examine the company, identify the key variables required to achieve the next stage, and then focus their presentation on those variables, why they are important, and how they will be accomplished. What a company says is important, but it also shows the management team's thinking process and judgment.

The most important management characteristic is judgment, which really goes to experience. Somebody who has done lots of things but has not learned how to draw from lessons learned through past experiences and projects really doesn't have what is required. With good judgment throughout an organization, the people in the organization will be able to have autonomy. The result is a company that is fast, nimble, and reactive to events. SBV spends a great deal of time in the due diligence process talking to every key member of the team.

Valuing a Company

SBV has internal guidelines against which we measure potential investments. Going forward, we look for an internal rate of return from the first investment of 35 percent per year until the liquidity event. So far, only Nanogram Devices, the implantable batteries company, has exceeded that target. We look for such a high return because we recognize how difficult creating a new start-up company and a technology is. The risks are so large that accomplishing the business plan on schedule is highly unlikely. If we make our target high enough to start with, we hope to end with an acceptable return even with the inevitable issues and problems.

Certainly rigorous financial modeling and discounted cash flow analysis exist for valuing companies. However, in a sense all the modeling and analysis really supports a decision, rather than leading to a decision. In the last several years, not much venture capital money has gone into companies. The price to invest in a company, therefore, has been low. Once venture capitalists begin to invest more, valuations will increase due to competition to invest in companies.

Over the past thirty to forty years of doing venture-backed companies in Silicon Valley, we have collectively come up with a pretty good model that includes percentile ranges that will be owned at an IPO date by the financial investors, by the CEOs and each of the vice presidents, in general by the employee group, and so on. We tend to shift around within ranges but not go wildly outside of those ranges. If we are likely to be widely outside of those ranges, the deal probably won't get done at all.

Spotting Opportunity in an Industry

Some venture capitalists have publicly said that they think of an opportunity and then go looking for a company that fits the idea, or maybe create a company that fits it. I am not smart enough to do that. What I know how to do is look at business plans and sift out the ideas where I would like to help accomplish a vision. Often, though, I don't think that what is described will create a lot of value, so I recommend some variations on the basic idea and work collaboratively with the team to revise the vision. Most people that are involved in the high-tech world, whether as venture capitalists, entrepreneurs, or whatever, love what we do because we get to think about what might be accomplished; we get to help create a new world.

Dealing with the Risks

SBV does not focus on the risks themselves, but rather on whether we believe we can overcome the risks. Every company will have huge risks. In all candor, if we focus just on the existing risks, we would probably never invest in anything because the risks are always so large. Also, we recognize that if we properly focus on getting the right people, with the strong academic and business backgrounds that have shown that they can translate what they've learned into the real world, then we can be fairly certain that we can overcome technical hurdles.

If the risks are market-based risks, such as not knowing if a particular product is likely to have a market at all, we probably won't invest. Other venture capitalists, especially those that have marketing backgrounds, are better able to internalize those marketing risks. We are much better at focusing on the business risks and the technology risks. Since we can understand those risks and their solutions, those are the risks we are more likely to be willing to adopt.

Frequent Entrepreneur Mistakes

Far and away, the most common mistake entrepreneurs make is trying to do too much themselves. Even though entrepreneurs often recognize that this is the biggest trap to avoid, they often still fall into the trap. Often, the entrepreneur will see something that needs to be done right away and he or she knows that he or she can do it more efficiently and faster than anyone in the company and just does it. This prevents the people in the rest of the organization from learning how to accomplish those day-to-day tasks, which would free the CEO to focus on the future and the strategy. Perhaps the biggest thing that a new CEO has to learn is how to force the organization around him or her to grow so that he or she can grow also.

The dollars and cents mistakes are common, as well. The optimists, people who believe that they can move mountains because they have moved mountains in the past, are always certain that things will take less time and money than they actually need. We, as the investors, need to make sure that timelines are flexible enough and bank accounts are big enough that when inevitable slips occur, they don't kill the company. In essence, we encourage the management team to be optimistic, while creating a safety net so that the company does not fail if everything is not perfect.

Frequent Venture Capitalist Mistakes

Falling in love with a company in which we have invested is very easy, whether it's with the technology, the promise of what is being created, or the marketing dream. We have to avoid falling in love with portfolio companies so we can see what is really happening in the company. If we are just focused on the dream, we will never take the difficult step to shut down or cut back a failing company. Far too often companies are kept open until they run out of cash. Getting the investors their money back isn't the only concern; freeing the resources tied up inside a failed company should also be a goal. The smart people involved with the failed company can offer society more if they are freed from the company to go work in a company with more opportunities.

Venture capitalists also regularly forget that their expertise is in investing in private companies. Holding onto IPO stock too long is a mistake and is often damaging to investors.

Becoming a Successful Venture Capitalist

When one of the premier venture capital organizations was first created, its bylaws required that general partners must have experience as a CEO of a company. Occasionally, they had people they wanted to recruit because they knew they would make great general partners of venture capital funds but they hadn't been a CEO. To meet the bylaw requirement, the partners would make the candidate a temporary CEO of a company in the portfolio just to force them to get that experience. While that organization has since changed its bylaws, CEO experience is probably the single most important quality needed for anyone wanting to work with embryonic companies.

The CEO is the guy that lies awake at night and wonders if he'll have enough money in the bank next week to pay the salary for twenty-five employees. Until a manager has experienced actually being a CEO, he or she does not really understand being responsible for an entire organization.

I often get letters or emails from M.B.A. students that want to become venture capitalists. I reply to them that the best thing they can do is start a company and run it. Succeed or fail, either way they will learn what it is like to run a company. Then they have a chance of being ready to deal with CEOs and of developing the judgment to apply their training to the companies in the portfolio.

Graham Burnette is a general partner of SBV Venture Partners, the third fund in the Euro-America family of funds. SBV is an early stage venture fund based in San Mateo, CA. Prior to joining SBV, he was chief operating officer and member of the board of directors of HolonTech, a company he co-founded in 1996. He built the company from a small engineering team into a corporation with sixty-five employees, shipping products at a $6 million/year revenue run-rate, at which time Lucent purchased its technology. HolonTech was a portfolio company of an earlier Euro-America fund.

From 1992 to 1996, Mr. Burnette was chief financial officer and vice president for business development at Mercury Interactive, another Euro-America portfolio company. Upon joining Mercury, Mr. Burnette implemented spending controls, a strategic planning system and information system, bringing the company to profitability, and a cash-flow positive situation in five months. He managed Mercury's IPO on Nasdaq fifteen months after joining the company, then ran all interactions with public market investors and business alliances for three years after the IPO.

Prior to his tenure with Mercury, Mr. Burnette was a corporate attorney with the firm of Wilson, Sonsini, Goodrich & Rosati in Palo Alto from 1987 to 1992. At WSGR, he provided both legal and business advice for high-growth technology-based companies, with particular emphasis on business alliances, public and private financings, mergers and acquisitions, technology in-licensing and out-licensing, and corporate governance.

Mr. Burnette holds degrees from the University of Virginia School of Law (J.D. 1986) and from the University of Virginia Graduate School of Business Administration (M.B.A. 1986) in Charlottesville, Virginia and a B.S. in commerce from Washington and Lee University in Lexington, Virginia (1982).

Exit, Stage Right

Gerard H. Langeler

General Partner
OVP Venture Partners

As an entrepreneur, you are the lead actor in a play only you can write. Be ready for your lines. Know your position on the stage, and know when and how to exit.

We always tell our portfolio companies, "If someone offers you money, find a way to take it." When opportunity knocks, you have to be very sure of your future to simply say "No, thank you." Perhaps another way to say this is, "If you are at the right stage, take the exit!"

OVP has been in the early stage venture capital business for over twenty years, investing in pre-revenue companies across the range from computational biology, drug discovery, medical devices to enterprise software, communications, and semiconductors. While there are clearly many differences in the product and market orientations of these firms, there are some constants as well. In fact, the pattern recognition that comes from seeing so many fledgling enterprises encounter similar challenges is what allows us to be a value added player around the board table.

When we meet with a startup, one of the first things we tell them is, lose the term "exit" from your business plan and your PowerPoint pitch. This is about liquidity, not an exit. Exit implies an end so that you can wrap up the package nice and neat, and be on your way. Not so!

If the liquidity event is an initial public offering (IPO), it is not an exit. In fact, it is just the beginning. The pressures of living in the public market fishbowl, particularly post-Sarbanes-Oxley, are enormous. The scrutiny you face from accountants, regulators, and shareholders can be daunting. Going public can be rewarding for your shareholders and your employees. It can help you achieve the goal of building a company of lasting value, if that is your goal. But it requires nerves of steel and a commitment to the company for the indefinite future. If you decide to sell your stock to the public, you need to fully internalize that there are now thousands of stakeholders counting on your performance. Don't let them down by looking for a quick "exit."

If the liquidity event is an acquisition by a public company, it may look like an "exit." Do not be confused. The acquiring company expects to receive value for their cash or stock. That value is not just measured at the time of the closing, but going forward. You should expect to join the acquiring firm and be locked into an employment contract for a number of years. You should expect to have some portion of the purchase price locked up in escrow—to be released only if what they "bought" turns out to be what you "sold." And, at times, there may well be an earn-out that requires specific deliverables over time before the liquidity becomes real.

Remember, in a play the only time an actor doesn't make it to the end of the performance is if they get killed off en route. Be ready to go the distance.

Start With a Clean Script

Great playwrights know how the story will end before they write the first scene. There isn't lots of scrambling around at the end of the performance to tie up loose ends. One similarity for startups is to keep your financial house in order from Day One. Realize that there will come a time where you will need clean financials, a clean capitalization table, and clean contracts. If you never let them become "dirty," you will have little to do when it comes time to prepare.

So what does "clean" mean in this context? First and foremost, it means doing everything in your power to be not just on the right side of the line of legality and ethics, but so far on the right side of that line that it is not even in view. We've all seen reports in the press of executives and investment professionals who crossed the line, some I'm convinced quite by accident. But they set themselves up by walking too close to it in the first place.

It means evaluating every transaction with the test that you would not be embarrassed if it showed up on the front page of your local newspaper. It means being a company you would want to invest in, even if you weren't part of it. In the area of capital structure, this means a simple, straightforward equity model, with investors few enough in number that you can name them all. As one of my colleagues once said sagely, "With a couple of individual investors you have angels. With a dozen, you have hell." A capitalization table with common stock and options for management and preferred stock for investors makes sense. A mishmash of many classes of stock, complex voting rights, convertible debt, and mysterious warrants adds up to a nightmare when it comes time to get everyone around the table to agree on a liquidity opportunity.

Timing Is Everything

On stage, good timing makes the difference between lines falling flat and a play coming to life. But that timing is at least under the actor's control. In biotech exits, timing has every bit as much to do with those providing the liquidity (IPO or merger/acquisition) as it does with what you are doing. The "right stage" is in the eye of the beholder. We have a house rule in our partnership: "Sell when the customer wants to buy."

There are two great points to realizing liquidity in any start-up business. First, when the business is all promise and no problems, and second, when the business is all progress and proven promise. The difficulty is that the period between point one and point two is often measured in three to five years. Once the initial promise period is passed and the problems all startups encounter are evident, there is often a sustained drop in the perceived value.

Biotech firms can usually find liquidity possibilities sooner in the process of product development. On the other hand, they often need to, given the capital intensity of the space.

There are two optimal times to seek liquidity—from an inside perspective and from an outside point of view.

From the inside: When there is enough meat on the bones of the promise that someone else can see what could be, without having to deal with what is. For example, this time period might come when phase one or two clinical trials are complete, but before the critical phase three period, or even before the reality of building a sales channel stares you in the face. The second point of time would be post phase three, with good customer uptake and a nice revenue ramp. You don't need profits but a clear path to profits—continuing already evident trends—is paramount.

From the outside: There are times when the public markets will pay you for showing up. In the biotech world, these windows seem to open every three to four years. When the window opens, you should go through it even if you aren't at one of the points mentioned above. That low cost of capital will likely not be repeated in a relevant time frame for you. The right stage is the stage at which you can accumulate a war chest of cash to see you through the trials ahead. However, don't confuse going public with being successful.

There are also times when market consolidation is in vogue, and large public companies will take you off the street to either boost their product portfolio, or at a minimum, keep a competitor from doing so. The important issue here is to view this as a game of musical chairs. It is best to grab a chair early. The longer the game goes on, the less likely you are to get a chair with large sums of cash attached. Usually, the first and second player to get consolidated (acquired) get paid. After that, you are lucky to get significant value.

You should try to find a situation where more than one acquirer views you not just as interesting, but as strategic. At that point, traditional methods of valuation are tossed aside in favor of the heat of the bidding process.

Valuation depends entirely on the market conditions at the time and the potential alternatives available to both parties. For example, my firm was the seed investor and later took Rosetta Inpharmatics (NASDAQ: RSTA) public at a time when it made sense—at about $350M market value. The company was sold to Merck for $600M one year later. Merck realized we didn't need them because we had cash from our IPO, but they needed us because our product was essentially one of a kind. Change either of those conditions, and the valuation immediately drops more than 50 percent.

Regardless of your path to liquidity, it usually helps to have a knowledgeable investment banker involved at the beginning of your process. In general, the first step is to look at comparable deals in recent times. They form the context in which your transaction will take place. That said, in this as in every other transaction, it is about the power of the buyer versus the power of the seller.

The Plot Thickens

We all know how tension rises as a play nears its climax. For your investors and yourselves, liquidity certainly qualifies as a climax point. When the liquidity event is complete, the preferred shareholders get paid first and then proceeds are distributed to management and shareholders according to their holdings. Vested options are treated as active holdings assuming the option price is paid. Unvested options are sometimes accelerated and sometimes not. In an M&A deal, often the acquiring company has a strong interest in either keeping the unvested shares in place, as "golden handcuffs," or will refresh the options of key employees they want to retain in the new parent firm. If everyone understands the sequence and processes here, tension will be kept to a minimum.

Now that the stock is in your investors' hands, what happens? Studies have shown that the best returns have been gained by VCs who sell "blindly" after the IPO or merger lockup expires (often 180 days) versus those who think they can outsmart the public markets. Now, blindly doesn't mean stupidly—as in dumping all the equity on an unsuspecting market where the company's stock is thinly traded. The best model seems to be a 25/25/50 percent pattern in which the VCs initially sell or distribute a quarter of their holdings, let that stock get absorbed into the market, and then proceed with another quarter a bit later. Having now liquidated half of their position, and possibly helped increase the daily trading volume in the security, often the last 50 percent can be sold all at once without upsetting the stock price.

This model, modified, makes equal sense for entrepreneurs. Once your lockup or restrictions have been lifted, you can start to consider how to turn those paper profits into cash. If you have gone public, expect strict "trading windows" which only allow you to buy or sell your company's security during specified times. For many firms, those times revolve around the thirty days after each quarterly earnings announcement, when there is an implicit assumption that the public knows all the material issues regarding company performance and financials. This then avoids both the reality and perception of any insider trading behavior. But be forewarned, *if* there is material information that is not public (and materiality gets measured retrospectively), you might not be able to trade even within the approved window. As a public company officer, I once went well over a year without seeing an open window for trading. When it did finally open and I chose to sell, there was a flurry of e-mail around the company wondering if this was a bad sign.

For that reason, I recommend the Bill Gates model of diversification and liquidity for entrepreneurs. Long ago, after Microsoft went public, Mr. Gates announced he was going to very slowly and systematically liquidate his Microsoft stock position. He went so far as to provide a range as to the percentage of his stock he planned to sell each year (5 to 10 percent if memory serves me). For years now, he's followed the program. At first, there were comments in the press such as, "Gates is selling. It must be a bad sign for Microsoft." However, over time, he continued selling and Microsoft continued growing to the point that now his quarterly stock dispositions don't even get mentioned. Could he have optimized his selling timing better? Certainly. Would that have been beneficial to his company? Not a chance. What he did was disassociate his desire for diversification and liquidity from his attitude about his company. It was a wise move. Bill made sure his character didn't get in the way of the play being successful.

When Ad Libs are Required

Up to now, we've talked about liquidity and exits in the context of good things happening. But that is not always the situation at hand. What about when things don't go as planned? When the company is not successful? What do you do then?

When a company has run out of cash, and there are no additional funding strategies, there are really very few options. In reality, you really don't want to ever go there. In a fire sale, it is only the seller who gets burned. You should look ahead and plan an exit—even a "bad" one—before you are left in this position. We all revel in stories of entrepreneurs who, like Lazarus, came back from the dead or near dead. Remember we talk about them because they are rare, not common. If you see the trends going against you and cash diminishing rapidly, look to find a buyer before it is clear to them (and your employees) that you need one. You may not get paid much, and you may feel in the end you wasted years of your life trying to build something substantial, but getting something is better than nothing. We've seen many deals where the entrepreneurs' intransigence prevented a modest liquidity event from happening, leading to a total wipeout.

If you can't find a buyer you should try to get a strategic partner to take a minority position, or work with suppliers and customers to provide financing. This strategy is really a long shot. Make sure you've exhausted all options before you bring the curtain down.

Take a Bow

With a lot of hard work and a bit of luck, you'll be looking at one of the good exits one of these days. Remember to take the exit when you can, not when you need to. The simple truth is, unlike in the world of sports, the business game does not have a straightforward clock. If you build something of lasting value, you will get to share in some of that value. The value you created took time. The value you delivered will play out over time, as will the value you receive. If you go onto the stage of the biotech startup with the mind-set that you are in it not for the exit, but for the journey, you will find yourself facing liquidity with a sense of satisfaction that transcends cash. But take the cash anyway.

Break a leg!

Gerard H. Langeler has spent the last dozen years as a general partner with OVP Venture Partners, a leading venture capital firm focused on high technology startups in the Pacific Northwest, with over $500 million of capital under management. The firm focuses on early stage software, communications, and computational biology infrastructure companies. Since 1983, the partnership has backed about eighty startups—and seen twenty-two of those achieve IPOs, with many others being acquired by public companies. From 1981 to 1992, Mr. Langeler was co-founder of Mentor Graphics Corporation where he served as president. He helped lead Mentor to over $400M in sales and $1B in market capitalization, ranking it as one of the largest and most profitable of all U.S. companies founded in the 1980s. His service as a board member covers the range from medical devices, enterprise software, network security, wireless communications to complex avionics. He is the author of The Vision Trap (Harvard Business Review, 3/92), which continues to be widely used in business schools and corporate training sessions. He holds an *A.B., chemistry from Cornell University, and a M.B.A. from Harvard. He currently serves on the board of directors of Max-Viz.*

Mr. Langeler serves as school board chair of the Riverdale School District. He previously chaired the Riverdale School Foundation. He also has served as chair of the Oregon Museum of Science & Industry (OMSI) Board of Trustees, and chair of the State of Oregon Health, Housing, Educational and Cultural Facilities Authority, a bonding agency for not-for-profits.

The Role of Counsel in Early Stage Equity Financings

Charles D. Powell

Partner

Haynes and Boone, LLP

The role of outside counsel changes dramatically as entrepreneurs move up the ladder from early stage financing to a mature company. Early in a company's life cycle, the need for comprehensive legal advice is fundamental and clients tend to look to their professionals as trusted advisors providing a broad range of experience, practical business advice, and recommendations. For example, in transactions with initial venture and angel capital, the entrepreneur may seek counsel to not only prepare the legal documents, but to also guide him in negotiating market and business terms, as well as assist in the identification and selection of other advisors. These areas of guidance may include:

- *Strategic Scope.* When counsel sits down with the entrepreneur for the first time they will have a broad discussion on the right way to structure the specific deal but also discuss the company's long-term needs for financing. Should the company offer preferred stock or common stock? What is selling now in the market? What are valuations like for similar companies? Selection of one type of financing early in the process may preclude alternative structures in the future.

- *Structure.* Counsel should have a strong opinion on what the market expects from a legal standpoint. A client would not want someone who is an expert on selling municipal bonds to work on a transaction for a technology startup. Aside from the serious consequences of utilizing an inexperienced advisor/counsel, inexperience in the practice areas will result in higher costs because of the necessary learning curve on unfamiliar documents. An entrepreneur should hire a professional with specific expertise in the area of representing startups and define what the specific expectations would be, what the fees are, and how the timing will work.

- *Contacts.* Companies hire lawyers many times for access to the attorney's rolodex. In other words, they should not only hire counsel, but also access to their counsel's network of contacts. Early stage companies are a clean slate as far as external relationships. The three sides of the relationship triangle in the world of early stage capital are: (i) companies seeking advice and capital, (ii) advisors (such as professional firms) who provide advice and referrals to capital, and (iii) capital sources referring service providers to companies and companies to service providers.

How Do Attorneys Decide to Work with a Company?

Lawyers look at early stage company representations in much the same way as venture capitalists decide whether to invest in a potential investment opportunity. They do not look for a billable hour opportunity, but instead look for a successful company to partner with from initial venture capital financing through an initial public offering. Accordingly, since a long-term relationship is envisioned, the credibility and capability of the company's management is crucial.

First, counsel will evaluate the source of the new business. Is it coming from a respected investment firm or another law firm? The association with (and the aura of) credible referral sources helps bridge the inevitable credibility gap experienced by entrepreneurs.

Next counsel will seek to determine what other professional service providers have worked with this company. Is there an accounting firm involved (which will add a lot of weight and credibility)? Who has done their compliance work? A serious alarm would be raised if a company has utilized (and fired) multiple law firms.

Finally, the lawyer will also investigate the backgrounds of the individuals involved in the company. Most people involved in these transactions have some business track record, and you can generally find people involved in other deals with them in the past. What was their last transaction? Who were the investors and who were the directors? A history of managers ending up in litigation with investors would send up red flags. Finally, an examination of the Securities and Exchange Commission database would occur.

Important Decisions in the Funding Process

In venture capital and early stage private equity angel transactions, the investors require and build into the documents provisions that protect their economic stake.

Valuation and Capitalization. Venture capital investors spend a significant amount of time understanding the business prospects of a company with an ultimate goal of obtaining the best valuation relative to such prospects. Valuation coupled with the capitalization of the company provides the ownership percentage of the parties. Entrepreneurs often misunderstand the different categories of common stock contained in the capitalization and will fail to appreciate that their stake and that of the other founders will include future grants to employees. For example, a typical capitalization requiring a 10 percent employee pool is as follows:

	Pre Money		Post Money	
	No. of Shares	%	No. of Shares	%
Founders	800,000	100%	900,000	40%
Employees	-	-	100,000	10%
Future Restricted Grants & Options				
Investors	-	-	1,000,000[1]	50%[1]

[1] Assumes $1 million pre money value of the company.

An entrepreneur in this example might assume that a $1,000,000 valuation would result in 800,000 shares issued to investors in a $1,000,000 raise (a 50/50 split in equity). However, investors calculate their percentage ownership on a "fully diluted basis" (i.e., the share base for calculating the investor's percentage will include issued shares, as well as future issuances pursuant to options, etc.). Therefore, VC firms will insist that they not be diluted by future employee grants, thus resulting in the founders retaining only 40 percent of the company.

Control. Control mechanisms are of supreme importance because they dictate the direction of the business. There are two levels of control. One is through control of the board and the other is through legal approval rights of investors for certain transactions (e.g. veto rights to block important transactions). VCs tend to see the latter as a backstop protection. However, entrepreneurs do not always realize the full impact of approval rights/restrictions covenants. They get a couple of years down the road and the investor does not let them do something they want to do, because there is a restrictive covenant that prevents them from doing it. For example, a typical restrictive count will prevent the sale of the company without the investors' consent. An investor with a $1,000,000 investment may not agree to a $2,000,000 sale.

Effective counsel will try to walk companies through the situations that could occur. Key issues faced by entrepreneurs are outlined on the Series A investment term sheet attached as Appendix A.

Term Sheet Legal Issues

Binding or Non Binding. The term sheet, or letter of intent, outlines the framework of the investment terms. Most parties will not want the term sheet to be legally binding, particularly the investor. The investor will want to be able to go in and do due diligence.

Type of Security. Preferred stock is the vehicle of choice for investors in investments in technology companies. Investment is through convertible preferred stock which allows the investor to retain significant and superior rights to the founders and management of the company, but also allows the investors the opportunity to convert their investment to common equity when the transaction appears successful. These superior rights range from preferred dividends to preferences on liquidation to mechanisms for shifting control of the board of directors.

Voting Rights. Preferred stock investors hold rights to vote with common shareholders on an "as converted" basis. Thus, the effect of antidilution provisions will result in greater control without the necessity of actual conversion. Voting rights for preferred stockholders will ensure that they maintain representation on the board and may provide for a shift of control from the common shareholders and founders to the preferred stockholders upon certain events of default or dilutions in later rounds. For instance, the failure to redeem the shares of preferred stock may result in a default, thereby providing super voting rights to investors. More importantly, though, the voting rights will ensure that the preferred stockholders are required to approve virtually any material strategic transaction. Their approval will be required prior to restructuring the business of the company, incurring indebtedness senior to the preferred stock or adding new investors to the company who may have rights senior or pari passu with the preferred stock.

Dividends. Preferred stock terms will often include a fixed or mandatory preferential dividend. In a distress situation, dividend provisions will take on significance because no distributions or dividends are allowed to be made to any other series of stock without payment of the preferential dividend to the venture capital investors. Also, please note that under Delaware General Corporation Law §170 dividends are not allowed to be paid unless the company has generated a surplus from operations or unless there is adequate capital surplus available for distribution. Because of the losses experienced by technology companies and their limited operating revenues, such entities are generally in a negative shareholders' equity position. Therefore, a payment of dividends is not possible.

Redemption. Preferred stock terms may include provisions requiring the company to redeem the preferred stock in certain situations, including at specific dates or upon default under covenants contained in the preferred stock instrument. The redemption of shares is subject to similar restrictions regarding surplus capital as is the case in preferred stock dividends. However, the failure of the company to redeem shares as required under mandatory redemption provisions may trigger cascading defaults potentially resulting in a change of control of the company and ultimately its liquidation.

Liquidation Preference. In a case of imminent failure or liquidation of a company, the liquidation preference will be the provision most likely revisited by the management of the company and its board of directors because it provides for the investors to receive "first dollars" out of the company upon its liquidation. However, since the preferred shares are equity and subordinate to any debt of the company (although senior to the common equity), these provisions can only be implemented once all debts, including accounts payable, are discharged and paid. Venture capitalists who participate in a distribution in violation of the rights of creditors subject themselves to personal liability. These provisions are most misunderstood by companies and founders and are frequently utilized by investors in distress situations. They ensure that subsequent rounds of investment capital, including down rounds and distress rounds, do not operate to affect the essential elements of the economic deal (viewed in its most favorable light) struck by the venture capitalists at the early stages of a technology company's life.

Antidilution. Antidilution rights are confusing as well. How is the investor's economic position (and valuation) protected in the event shares are issued for a price less than the investor's purchase price? There can be some dramatic differences in the way you handle that situation. In one extreme, investors may request what is called a "full ratchet protection," which means the price for converting their shares to common stock drops to the lowest point that shares were ever issued or the parties may arrive at a "weighted average" solution for down rounds.

The most difficult provision for a company, the "full ratchet" antidilution right, will allow the preferred stock conversion or "strike" price to float, or "ratchet," down to the lowest level of any subsequent financing, without regard for the level of new investment. For example, assume that in 2003 a venture capitalist invested $5 million, at $1.00 per share, convertible on a one-to-one basis to common stock of a new company. At the time of the initial investment, the company has a $15 million valuation resulting in the investor holding 25 percent of the company (5 million shares on an "as converted" basis). In 2004, the company is in a distress mode and in order to survive and make September payroll, is required to raise $100,000 at $.10 a share (convertible to 1,000,000 shares). Under a full ratchet, the preferred stock investor's $5 million position would automatically readjust to a conversion ratio of $.10 a share. Obviously, the dilution from a transaction of this type would be massive. The venture capitalists would now have the right to convert their $5 million in preferred stock to 50 million shares and possess total control of the company. This result would be accomplished even though the new investor had only put in a relatively small amount of money (e.g., $100,000).

In contrast, the weighted average alternative simply provides for an adjustment of the venture capital investor's strike price based upon a moving scale of the price paid by the new investor related to their total investment. Accordingly, a small investment relative to the first round will have a minor impact on the conversion rights of the initial investors.

For example, if a future transaction was effected at a price lower than the initial investor's purchase price, the investor's conversion price would be lowered (and the founder's correspondingly diluted) in accordance with the following formula:

$$CP_2 = CP_1 * (A+B) / (A+C)$$

CP_2 = New Conversion Price

CP_1 = Conversion Price in effect immediately prior to new issue

A = Number of shares of Common Stock deemed to be outstanding immediately prior to new issue (includes all shares of outstanding common stock, all shares of outstanding preferred stock on an as-converted basis, and all outstanding options on an as-exercised basis; and does not include any convertible securities converting into this round of financing)

B = Aggregate consideration received by the Corporation with respect to the new issue divided by CP_1

C = Number of shares of stock issued in the subject transaction

Generally, an entrepreneur and his counsel will attempt to carve out certain transactions from these potentially onerous provisions, such as:

- securities issued upon the conversion of any currently outstanding debenture, warrant, option, or other convertible security;
- common stock issuable upon a stock split, stock dividend, or any subdivision of shares of common stock;
- shares of common stock (or options to purchase such shares of common stock) issued or issuable to employees or directors of, or consultants to, the company pursuant to incentive plans approved by the company's board of directors; and
- shares of common stock issued or issuable to banks, equipment lessors pursuant to a debt financing, equipment leasing or real property leasing transaction.

Due Diligence

After material terms are agreed to, the heavy lifting by investors and their advisors come during the due diligence phase. See example of a typical due diligence checklist attached as Appendix B.

Standard practices include reading through their corporate records, their minute books, and their employment agreements. The problem often occurs that documents have not been created or transactions properly documented. Most entrepreneurs and early stage companies have verbal agreements and promises to people, many of which are not documented. If they have not documented the terms of their employees or consultants, they may have a glaring hole in their capital structure, or in the case of contractor and consultants, not even own the technology. It may be owned by someone else. Therefore, due diligence is really an examination of the company as a whole, especially what has been neglected.

The Challenge of IP

Intellectual property protection is constantly evolving. Key questions to ask:

- What is the company's patent position? How is it protected?
- Does the company have a patent strategy for protecting its technology?
- Is there someone else or other patents that may create a problem for the company?

VCs get excited when a company claims to possess patents and a proprietary position in a technology. Then they find out that the company has not filed proper documents and has lost their rights everywhere in the world except the U.S. and the filed patent has problems (i.e., coverage is not adequate for the company's business line). For example, we often run into situations where the company has a technology, the commercialization of which is dependent on a key set of software code. However, because the code was written by an outside contract developer, the company does not actually own the code. This unfortunate outcome results from inferior (or lack) of legal documentation specifying that the company will own a work product of the contractor.

Legal Issues with Debt

After March 2000, when the venture capital business determined that the capital markets would not rebound quickly to provide capital for expansion and liquidity, certain elements of early stage seed capital providers moved away from preferred stock to convertible debt structure. This movement was attributable in part to a desire to have absolute control in the situation of a failed enterprise and to be able to take the company, liquidate it, and take the assets to put someplace else.

We saw many transactions on a convertible debt basis (see Appendix C for typical convertible debt terms). This instrument is similar to preferred stock from a conversion feature but until that point, the investor is a creditor, and first in line as a creditor. If the enterprise is not successful, the investors can step in and take control of the assets of the company, liquidate, and protect their position.

From the founder's perspective in a preferred stock scenario, they had the ability, as long as control of the board was maintained, to retain ownership and control of the company. Shareholders, even if with redemption rights, are still stockholders at the most basic level and don't have the ability to make the company give them anything.

Convertible debt holders stand in a different position. They are secured creditors and they can foreclose upon and sell assets, depending on what state a company is in, without court authorization. It is a lot worse for the company and it moves the investors up the food chain to the top of the company's capital structure. If entrepreneurs have to agree to some sort of convertible debt structure, they should insist that it is unsecured and subordinated to current or future senior debt of the company.

Legal Issues with Angel Investors

Angel investors have adopted a legal approach similar to the venture capital model of investing. They want preferred stock and they want the kind of terms that a VC would get. The major legal issue is that they can get in your way when you go for your first round of professional financing. Angel investors are entrepreneurs. They are not professional investors but they do it as much for the ability to work with another entrepreneur and to mentor them. VCs are strictly bottom-line oriented. They are looking for the best deal, lowest price, get out in three to five years, and make a lot of money.

Angel investors have a notorious reputation for overpaying for companies because they don't have the internal back-office and infrastructure support that VCs have on valuing companies. The only term that they really spend a lot of time on is the valuation. They rely on their counsel, but as businessmen they will not be forestalled on board representation, anti-dilution, or liquidation preferences issues. They are more proactive in how they are going to be involved in the business.

If an entrepreneur intends to utilize angel investors, the goal for an entrepreneur should be to bring mentors in, people who are going to help build the business who have contacts and know the venture capital firms. The right angel investors have the right relationships in the particular technology area.

Other Issues

The two major issues in any financing are human resources and intellectual property ("IP"). Most technology companies have a key visionary or groups of visionaries that are essential to the business. It is a people-oriented intensive business. The investor also has to make sure that the value of the company doesn't leak out. They are really buying skills and knowledge in technology. Agreements with key people must be in place to make sure that they are not buying a skill set and expertise that can walk out the door six months from now and take the technology to somebody else.

The centerpiece to technology is patent/copyright protection for assets. Making sure that you are totally protected on the company's position is virtually impossible. You have to have good advisors. Those two items are the differentiators.

The intrinsic value of the assets is difficult to get your arms around. From the investor side, the keys are to understand the company's IP position and understand how it is protected, and to make sure the people whose brains control the IP are in place and can't drift off or take it with them. In the event things work out, you know what that technology is and you can potentially access it. The U.S. patent code and statutes all affect technology companies that are pretty much unregulated unless you are in telecommunications.

Conclusion

The entrepreneur starting down the fundraising road faces a myriad of complicated business and legal issues. What is the value of his business? What risk does he face by being an equity investor/venture capitalist and should he consider another mode of funding? Faced with the decision, the founder/chief executive officer should attempt to secure advisors who are able to bring broad advice to the business.

Charles D. Powell is the head of Haynes and Boone's technology practice in Houston and handles venture capital, securities offerings, mergers and acquisitions, and representation of technology companies including telecom companies and enterprises deploying technology in the energy industry.

Mr. Powell was lead counsel in the following matters:

- *Strategic investor in $23 million investment in a wireless company*
- *VC investor in $10 million telecom preferred stock investment*
- *$30 million venture capital investment in two telecom equipment manufacturers*
- *Energy service e-commerce company in its $60 million merger with an online well service and product procurement company*
- *Business-to-business energy service business in its VC financing*
- *NYSE seismic products manufacturer in $60 million preferred stock placement*
- *Long distance reseller in sale to national telecom company*
- *Energy technology issuer in connection with two rounds of VC funding and sale to a NYSE company*
- *Energy company in $100 million preferred stock placement and $1.2 billion restructuring of offshore deepwater business*
- *VC financing for radioactive pharmaceuticals business*
- *IPO of a computer company*
- *IPO of an oil well technology company*

Mr. Powell received his J.D. from the University of Texas in 1979 and his B.A. in history from Columbia University in 1976.

Dedication: *This chapter is dedicated to Rosemary Spear Powell (1925-2001).*

APPENDIX A

TERM SHEET

THIS TERM SHEET PROVIDES AN EXAMPLE OF A TYPICAL EARLY ROUND INVESTMENT IN PREFERRED STOCK. IT IS NOT INTENDED AS SPECIFIC LEGAL ADVICE OR A FINAL LEGAL DOCUMENT AND IS PROVIDED FOR GENERAL EDUCATIONAL PURPOSES ONLY.

XXX, INC.

TERMS OF SALE OF SERIES A PREFERRED STOCK

[This term sheet relates to a preferred stock equity investment. Investors may also invest in convertible debt or common stock. The choice of the form of investment revolves around a number of issues including control issues and liquidation priority. An investor in preferred stock may receive mandatory board representation as well as consent rights on material corporate matters (e.g., merger, sale of assets, etc.).

[_____, 2004]

XXX, Inc., a Delaware corporation (the "Company"), proposes a private placement of securities to certain individuals and entities (the "Investors"), on the terms set forth below.

Form of Investment: Convertible Series A Preferred Stock ("Series A").
[Common Stock] [Convertible Debt]

Valuation: $4,500,000

Investment Amount: $500,000

Capitalization:

	No. of Shares	Percentage
Founders	3,500,000	70%
Investors	500,000	10%
Option Pool	1,000,000[1]	20%

---

[1] Unissued reserve

[Note: That the investors' percentage is calculated on a "fully diluted" basis which includes unissued shares under employee options and warrants or employee options reserved for future issuance.]

Dividends:

The holders of the Series A shall be entitled to receive cumulative dividends of ___ percent (___%) per share per annum in preference to the Common Stock ("Common") when and if declared by the board of directors.

[Dividends are not likely to be paid early in a company's cycle because of a lack of earnings. The dividends provided here are cumulative in that unpaid dividends accumulate and are paid when the Company achieves earnings and the Board is able to pay dividends. The accumulated dividends will be required to be paid prior to any distributions to holders of Common.]

Liquidation Preference:

In the event of any liquidation or winding up of the Company (which shall include mergers, sales of substantially all of its assets, etc.), the holders of the Series A shall be entitled to receive in preference to the holders of Common an amount equal to $_____ per share (the "Original Purchase Price"), plus any declared and unpaid dividends. Any remaining proceeds shall be allocated between the Common and Series A on a pro rata basis, treating the Series A on an as-if-converted basis.

[The return to the investor provided above is known as "participating preferred" or a double dip return: (i) the return of face value and dividends, plus (ii) a distribution sharing with Common thereafter on an "as converted basis."

Conversion:

Each share of Series A may be converted at the holder's option at any time into one share of Common ("Conversion Stock"), subject to adjustment as described below. The Series A will be automatically converted to Common upon the closing of a public offering of more than $____ of Company stock for not less than $____ per share (subject to proportionate adjustment for future stock splits, dividends or combinations).

Conversion Price Adjustments:

The conversion price of the Preferred Stock shall be subject to adjustment proportionately for stock splits, stock dividends, recapitalizations, etc. and will be adjusted upon future "down" rounds on a weighted average basis.

[When future sales of stock are at a price less than the conversion price of the Series A, the holders of the Series A are protected through antidilution rights: "weighted" or "full ratchet." A "weighted average" antidilution provision reduces the price based on the relative amount of the new capital. In contrast, a "full ratchet" is a full adjustment of the conversion price to the lower price. For example, assume that the company issued 1,000,000 shares of preferred shares to an

117

angel group at $1.00 a share. A subsequent issuance of 100,000 shares to a third party at $.50 would result in the adjustment or "full ratchet" of the conversion price down to $.50 even though the actual economic dilution is not $.50 a share.]

Voting Rights:

The holder of each share of Series A shall have the right to that number of votes equal to the number of shares of Common issuable upon conversion of such share of Series A. The Series A votes together with the Common on all matters including election of directors.

Protective Provisions:

A majority of the Series A must approve (i) any amendment of the Articles of Incorporation which would change the authorized number of Series A or the rights, preferences, and privileges of the Series A or (ii) creation of shares having dividend or liquidation rights equal or superior to the Series A.

[This provision may also provide extensive other negative control rights to the Series A (e.g., required class approval of mergers, bank financings, stock repurchases, etc.).]

Registration Rights:

Demand Rights: If at any time, six months after the effective date of the Company's first underwritten public offering, investors holding at least 50 percent of the Series A or Conversion Stock request that the Company file a registration statement for an aggregate offering price of $____, the Company will use its best efforts to cause such shares to be registered. The Company shall not be obligated to effect more than two registrations under these demand right provisions.

"Piggyback" Registration: If at any time the Company determines to register its securities, the Series A holders shall be entitled to have their Conversion Stock included in such registration subject to underwriter reduction of piggyback shares based on market conditions.

S-3 Demand Rights: If available for use by the Company, the investors will be entitled to two S-3 registrations.

Preemptive Right: The holders of the Series A shall have the right to purchase all or any part of such holder's pro rata share of certain securities issued by the Company after the closing of the Series A transaction (the "New Securities"), on the same terms and at the same price at which the Company proposes to sell the New Securities.

Courtesy of Charles D. Powell, Haynes and Boone, LLP

APPENDIX B

DUE DILIGENCE CHECKLIST

In connection with the proposed transaction, please provide us with the following materials or information relating to Newco, Inc. and any subsidiaries (together, the "Company"). Upon review, we may request additional documents. If compiling any of the requested items would be unduly burdensome, please let us know so that we may arrange a less burdensome alternative.

A. **Corporate Documents of the Company and Subsidiaries**

1. Certificate of Incorporation and all amendments thereto, including proposed amendments.

2. Bylaws and all amendments thereto, including proposed amendments.

3. Minutes of all Board of Directors, committee, and stockholders meetings and all consents to actions without meeting.

4. List of states in which qualified to do business and in which the Company has offices, holds property or conducts business.

5. List of foreign countries in which doing business and a description of the Company's business activities.

6. Material information or documents furnished to stockholders and to directors during the last two years.

7. Most recently obtained good standing certificates for all states and countries where the Company is qualified to do business.

B. **Previous Issuances of Securities**

1. Sample copy of stock certificates, warrants, and options.

2. List of stockholders, indicating number of shares held, dates of issuance, consideration paid, and addresses of record and beneficial owners.

3. All stock option, stock purchase, and other employee benefit plans and forms of agreements.

4. List of outstanding stock options and warrants showing dates of issuance or grant, amounts issued or granted, exercise prices, exercise and expiration dates, vesting schedules, dates, and amounts of exercise and cancellation and optionees or holders.

5. Any voting trust agreements, buy/sell agreements, stockholder agreements, warrant agreements or proxies affecting the right of any stockholder to freely sell or vote shares of the Company.

6. Any registration rights or preemptive rights agreements.

7. Powers of attorney on any matter.

8. Convertible debt instruments.

9. Other contracts, arrangements, or public or private commitments relating to the stock of the Company to which any officer or director of the Company is a party or which involves more than 5 percent of the Company's Common Stock.

10. Any debt arrangements, guarantees or indemnification between officers, directors or principal (5 percent) stockholders and the Company.

11. Any other agreements relating to sales of securities by Company, including stock purchase agreements, private placement memoranda or other offering circulars.

C.   Material Contracts and Agreements

1.   List of banks or other lenders with whom Company has a financial relationship (briefly describe nature of relationship—lines of credit, equipment lessor, etc.).

2.   Credit agreements, debt instruments, security agreements, mortgages, financial or performance guaranties, indemnifications, liens, equipment leases or other agreements evidencing outstanding loans to which the Company is a party or was a party within the past two years involving more than $25,000.

3.   All material correspondence with lenders during the last three years, including all compliance reports submitted by the Company or its accountants.

4.   List the ten largest suppliers of the Company for each of the last two fiscal years and the latest interim period, indicating the types of products and amounts purchased from each and, if applicable, any sole source suppliers.

5.   Agreements with suppliers listed in (4) above.

6.   List of dealers and major customers and their locations.

7.   Copy of any sales agent or representative agreements.

8.   Any other material contracts.

D.   Litigation

1.   Copies of any pleadings or correspondence for pending lawsuits.

2.   Summary of disputes with suppliers, competitors, or customers.

3.   Correspondence with auditor regarding threatened or pending litigation, assessment or claims.

4. Correspondence concerning inquiries from federal or state tax authorities.

5. Decrees, orders or judgments of courts or governmental agencies.

6. Settlement documentation.

E. **Employees and Related Parties**

1. A management organization chart and biographical information.

2. Summary of labor disputes which have been referred to federal or state authorities.

3. Correspondence, memoranda or notes concerning pending or threatened labor stoppage.

4. List of negotiations with any group seeking to become the bargaining unit for any employees.

5. Collective bargaining agreements.

6. All employment and consulting agreements, loan agreements and documents relating to other transactions with officers, directors, key employees, and related parties.

7. Schedule of all compensation paid to officers, directors and key employees for most recent fiscal year showing separately salary, bonuses and non-cash compensation (i.e. use of cars, property, etc.).

8. Summary of employee benefits and copies of any pension, profit sharing, deferred compensation, and retirement plans.

9. Summary of management incentive or bonus plans not included in (8) above, as well as other non-cash forms of compensation.

10. Sample confidentiality agreements with employees.

11.   Indemnification agreements with officers, directors and employees.

12.   Description of all related party transactions that have occurred during the last five years (and any currently proposed transaction) and all agreements relating thereto.

F.   Financial Information

1.   Audited financial statements for the last three fiscal years.

2.   Quarterly income statements for the last fiscal year and current fiscal year to date.

3.   Financial or operating budgets or projections, with quarterly information for the last two fiscal years (and beyond, if any).

4.   Business plan and other documents describing the current and/or expected business of the Company including all material marketing studies, consulting studies or reports prepared by the Company.

5.   A description of all changes in accounting methods or principles during the last three fiscal years.

6.   Any documents relating to material write-downs or write-offs other than in the ordinary course during the last three fiscal years.

7.   Revenue, gross margin, and average selling price by product.

8.   Management letters or special reports by auditors and any responses thereto for the last three fiscal years.

9.   Letters of counsel to the Company delivered to auditors for the last three fiscal years.

10.   Detailed aging schedules for accounts receivable for the last two fiscal years.

11.   Detailed aging schedules for inventory for the last three fiscal years.

12. Detailed breakdown of G&A expenses for the last three fiscal years.

13. Backlog information.

14. Copies of any valuations of the Company's stock.

15. Description of all contingent liabilities.

16. Schedule of store openings and closings by month for the last three fiscal years and current fiscal year to date.

G.   Property

1. Schedule of leases.

2. List of real and material personal property owned by the Company.

3. Documents of title, mortgages, deeds of trust and security agreements pertaining to the properties listed in (1) above.

4. All outstanding leases with an original term greater than one year for real and personal property to which the Company is either a lessor or lessee including, but not limited to, offices, distribution centers, and warehouses.

5. Description of trademarks or pending applications, copyrights, trade secrets, and other intellectual property arrangements.

6. Documents pertaining to proprietary technology developed/owned by the Company, including any copyright or patent filings. This will also include information confirming that the Company's software and technology is owned by the Company and does not infringe on any other party's rights.

H.   Taxation

1.   Any notice of assessment, revenue agents' reports, etc. from federal or state authorities with respect to any currently "open" years.

2.   Federal and state income tax returns for the last six years.

I.   Insurance and Liability

1.   Schedule or copies of all material insurance policies of the Company covering property, liabilities and operations, including product liabilities.

2.   Schedule of any other insurance policies in force such as "key man" policies or director indemnification policies.

3.   All other relevant documents pertaining to the Company's insurance and liability exposure, including special reserve funds and accounts.

J.   Acquisition, Partnership or Joint Venture Agreements

1.   All acquisition, partnership or joint venture agreements.

2.   Documents pertaining to potential acquisitions.

3.   Any agreements regarding divestiture of divisions or assets.

4.   List and summary description of acquisitions in the past five years.

K.   Governmental Regulations and Filings

1.   Summary of OSHA inquiries for past three years.

2.   Summary of federal and state EPA, EEO, or other governmental agency inquiries during the past three years.

3.   Material reports to government agencies for past three years (e.g., OSHA, EPA).

4.   Copies of all permits and licenses necessary to conduct the Company's business.

5.   Summary of applicable federal, state and local laws, rules, and regulations.

L.   <u>Miscellaneous</u>

1.   Press releases during the last two years.

2.   Articles, analysts' reports, and other pertinent marketing studies or reports relating to the Company or the industry.

3.   Information regarding competitors.

4.   Customer satisfaction surveys, if any.

5.   Current brochures and sales materials describing the Company's products.

6.   Permits/licenses.

Courtesy of Charles D. Powell, Haynes and Boone, LLP

APPENDIX C

CONVERTIBLE DEBT TERMS

Company: Newco, Inc., a Delaware corporation.

Aggregate Amount of Debt: Up to $800,000.

Securities: Secured convertible debt (the "Convertible Debt") and warrants to purchase preferred stock of the Company (the "Warrants").

Security for Convertible Debt: Inventory, accounts, equipment, intangibles, proprietary assets, and investment property of the Company.

Drawdowns: $200,000 on September 30, 2004; $400,000 on December 31, 2004; $200,000 on February 28, 2005.

Closing Date: The Transaction will be made pursuant to definitive documents and instruments mutually satisfactory to the Company and the Lender; the date of the Convertible Loan and Security Agreement to be entered into by and among the Company and the Lenders is September 30, 2004 (the "Effective Date").

Maturity: March 31, 2005, if not converted prior thereto. All principal and accrued but unpaid interest may be convertible at the option of the holder prior to the closing of an "Acquisition" of the Company (as described below) or, in lieu of conversion, the holder may accelerate the indebtedness under its Note at the time of an Acquisition.

Interest: Eight percent (8%) per annum, with interest accruing on advances when made until maturity.

Convertibility: At any time within six months of the Effective Date all of the principal and any accrued but unpaid interest on the Convertible Debt may be converted at the option of the holder into shares of the Company's equity securities most recently issued and sold to third party investors at a conversion price equal to 70 percent of the purchase price paid by those investors.

After six months of the date of the Effective Date, the Convertible Debt may be converted at the option of the holder into shares of the Company's equity securities most recently issued and sold to third party investors at a conversion price equal to 50 percent of the purchase price paid by those investors.

Upon an Acquisition (defined as a sale of all or substantially all of the Company's assets, or a merger or consolidation or stock sale that results in pre-sale shareholders holding less than a majority of the voting power of the surviving corporation) the Convertible Debt is convertible on a dollar-for-dollar basis into shares of Common Stock at a conversion price equal to 80 percent of the lesser of the Common Stock equivalent price per share paid by the acquiring person in such Acquisition or the Common Stock equivalent price per share paid by the purchasers of the Company's capital stock in its most recent round of financing or negotiated purchase and sale of its capital stock.

Prepayment and The Company may prepay any amounts without
Mandatory Payment: penalty. The Company must repay the Convertible Debt (if not converted) upon the closing of a next preferred stock equity investment in the Company.

Non-Subordination: The Convertible Debt is not subordinate to other indebtedness of the Company.

Warrant Term:	Expires September 30, 2014.
Exercise Terms:	Exercisable for shares of preferred stock of the Company of the same class and series most recently issued and sold to third party investors (a "Subsequent Financing") or, if no Subsequent Financing occurs, shares of the Series A Convertible Preferred Stock.
Exercise Price:	If Series A Preferred Stock: $1.00 per share. If another series of preferred stock: The price per share paid by third party investors in that financing.
Number of Shares:	Determined by dividing the "Aggregate Exercise Price" by the applicable Exercise Price.
Aggregate Exercise Amount:	Two times (2x) the Convertible Debt amount loaned by the Lenders if Convertible Debt repaid within two months of issuance; one and one-half times (1.5x) the Convertible Debt loaned by the Lenders if Convertible Debt repaid within four months of issuance; and one times (1x) the Convertible Debt amount loaned by the Lenders if Convertible Debt repaid after four months of issuance.
Anti-Dilution Adjustments:	Full anti-dilution adjustments, including weighted average price protection for shares issued at or representing less than then-current fair market value or then-current exercise price.
Warrant Cashless Exercise Feature:	Customary provision included.

Courtesy of Charles D. Powell, Haynes and Boone, LLP

Other Venture Capital Books

- **Venture Capital Valuations** - Top VCs on Step by Step Strategies and Methodologies for Valuing Companies at All Stages - $99.95
- **Venture Debt Alternatives and Evaluation Guidelines** - A Comprehensive Look at the Venture Debt Marketplace Along With a Systematic Framework for Approaching the Debt Capital Markets, Increasing Transaction Transparency and Avoiding Common, Costly Mistakes. - $249.95
- **Pitching to Venture Capitalists** - Essential Strategies for Approaching VCs, Entering Into Negotiations and Securing Funding - Written by Leading VC Patrick Ennis - $49.95
- **Non-Disclosure Agreements (NDA) Line by Line** - A Detailed Look at NDA's, How to Change Them, and Contract Samples You Can Use - A Must Read Before Signing Any NDA or a Great Way to Update Your Current NDA - $99.95
- **Raising Capital for Biotech Companies** - An Insider's Guide to 300+ Keys to Successful Financings - $499.95
- **Deal Teams** - Roles and Motivations of Management Team Members, Venture Capitalists, Investment Bankers, Lawyers & More in Mergers, Acquisitions and Equity Investments - $27.95

Financial Modeling Tools in Excel

Ready to Use: VC Valuation Models for Private Companies - Interactive Excel Spreadsheet on CD-Rom - Document Can be E-mailed Immediately - Simply plug in the numbers as directed in the spreadsheet to quickly and easily arrive at your desired results – or customize the spreadsheet to make development easier. Written by top VC Praveen Gupta of CDIB Ventures, the spreadsheet provides two general methods to value a private company:

1) Desired Ownership: This scenario is typically applicable to pre-revenue companies. Many VC's have an internal strategy of owning certain minimum percentage of a company. Typically, it is 15-20 percent post funding in early stage companies. Once the investor has made the decision to invest, they have estimated the exit potential and returns for their investment.

2) Financial Ratios: This scenario may typically be applied to revenue stage companies. First scenario may still be applicable either entirely or partially. A public company is typically valued in multiple ways using various financial ratios. These include Price to Earnings (PE), Price to Sales (PS), Discounted Cash Flow (DCF), Shareholder equity, or a combination of these ratios. $99.95

Ready to Use: Dilution Models for Private Companies - Interactive Excel Spreadsheet on CD-Rom Created by Top VC Praveen Gupta - Document Can be E-mailed Immediately - Plug in your numbers as directed in the spreadsheet to quickly and easily arrive at your desired results – or customize the model to make development easier. The model allows you to analyze the dilution impact of a new equity offering as well as other events such as options, warrants, etc. The model contains the following worksheets:

1) Summary – Provides a summary of dilution for various methods
2) Pre-Money Cap-Table – Allows you to enter your current capitalization and information on the new equity offering
3) Following worksheets do not require any input but shows complete computation
a. No Adjustment – No adjustments are made to counter the dilution
b. Full Ratchet – Applies price adjustments based on Full-Ratchet method
c. Narrow – Applies price adjustments based on Narrow based weighted average method
d. Middle of Road – Applies price adjustments based on Middle of the Road based average method
e. Broad – Applies price adjustments based on Broad based weighted method. $499.95